A-Z Street Atlas of NORWICH

CW00409089

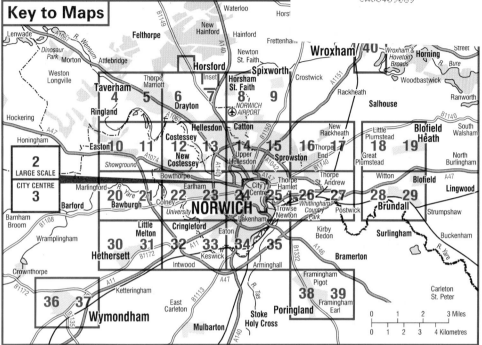

Reference

A Road	A11	**Footpath** …
Under Construction		**Residential Walkway** …
Proposed		**Railway** — Level Crossing / Station
B Road	B1108	**Built Up Area**
Dual Carriageway		**District Boundary**
One Way Street Traffic flow on A Roads is indicated by a heavy line on the drivers left.	→	**Posttown Boundary** By arrangement with the Post Office
Pedestrianized Road		**Postcode Boundary** Within Posttown
Restricted Access		**Map Continuation** 10
Track		**Ambulance Station**

Car Park Selected	P
Church or Chapel	†
Fire Station	■
Hospital	H
House Numbers A & B Roads only	113 / 98
Information Centre	i
National Grid Reference	145
Police Station	▲
Post Office	★
Toilet	▽
With Facilities for the Disabled	🚻

Scale

1:15,840
4 inches to 1 mile

0   ¼   ½   ¾ mile
0   250   500   750   1 kilometre

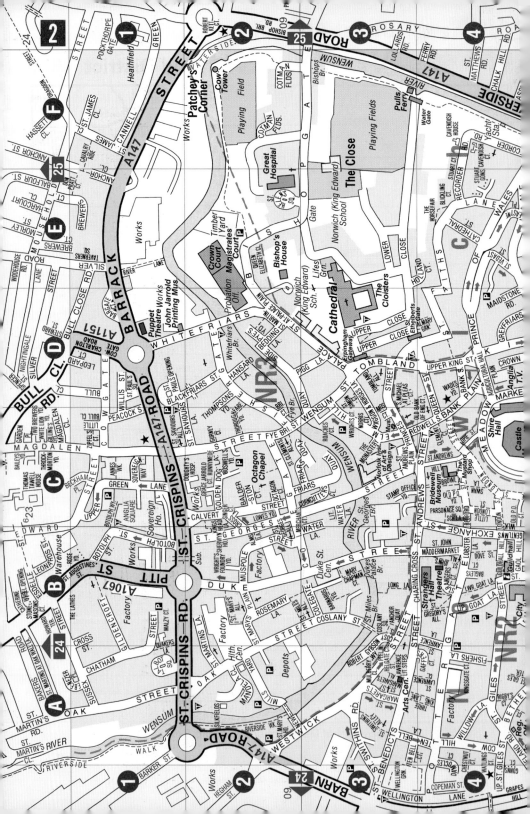

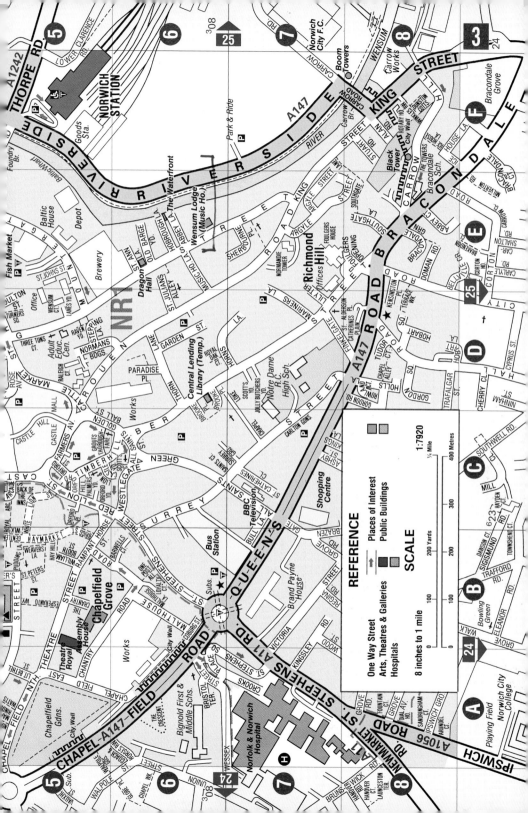

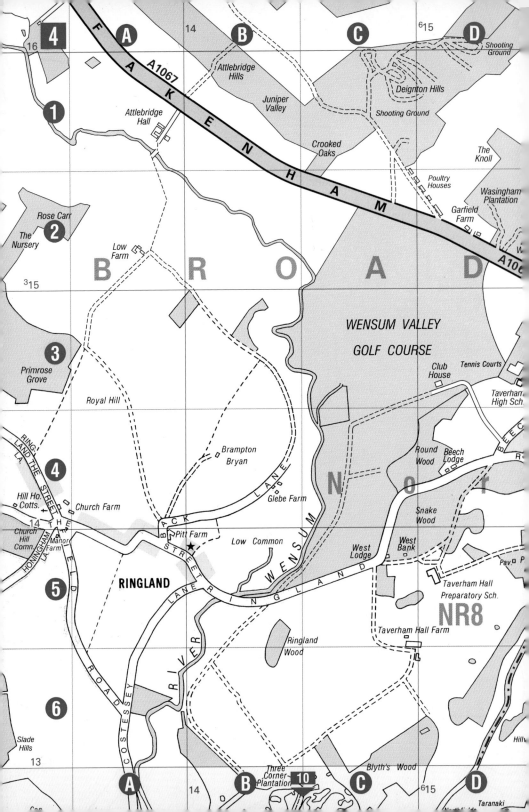

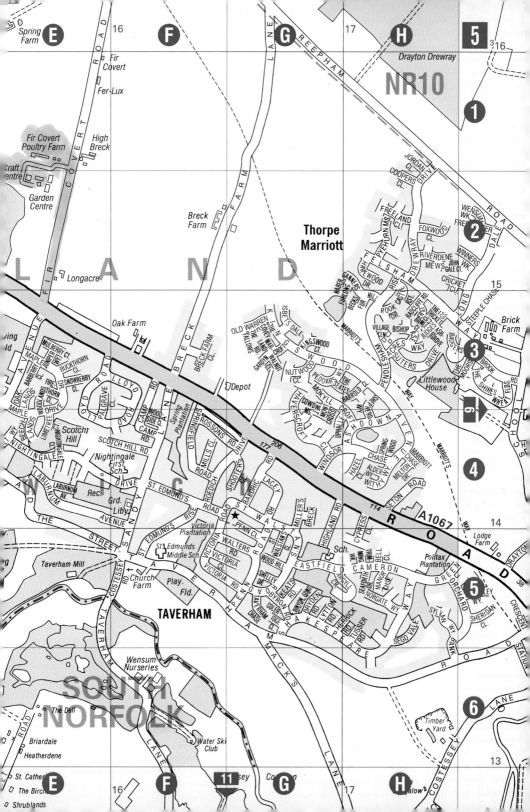

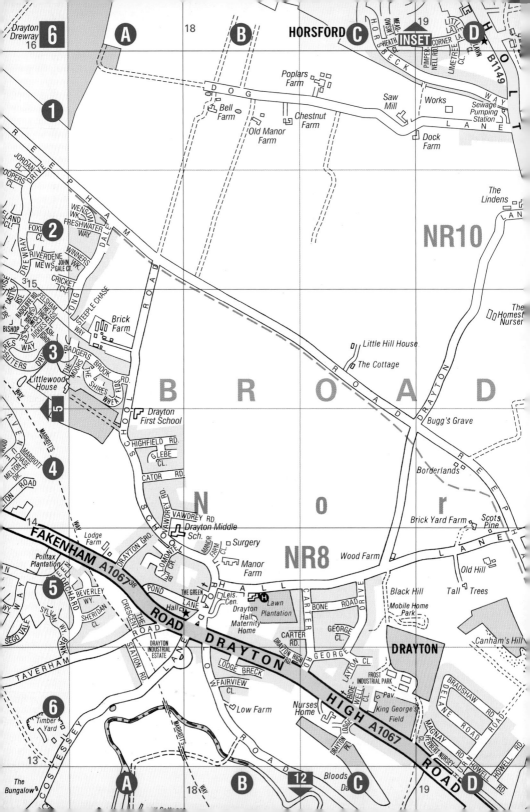

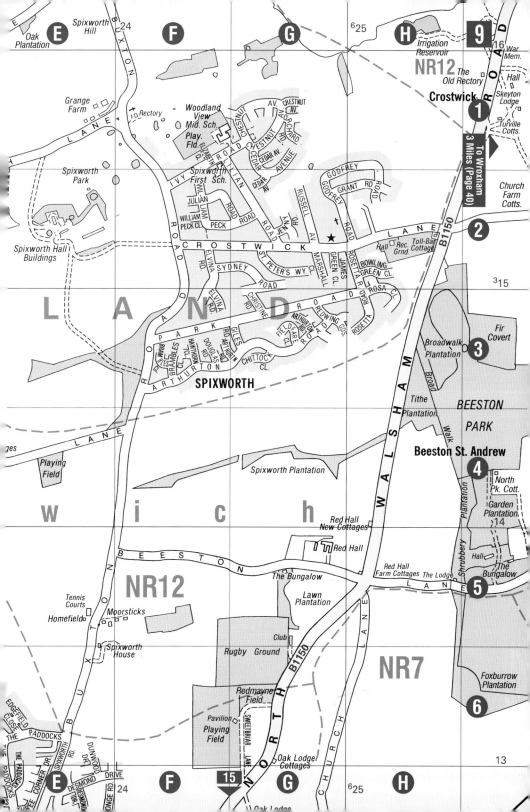

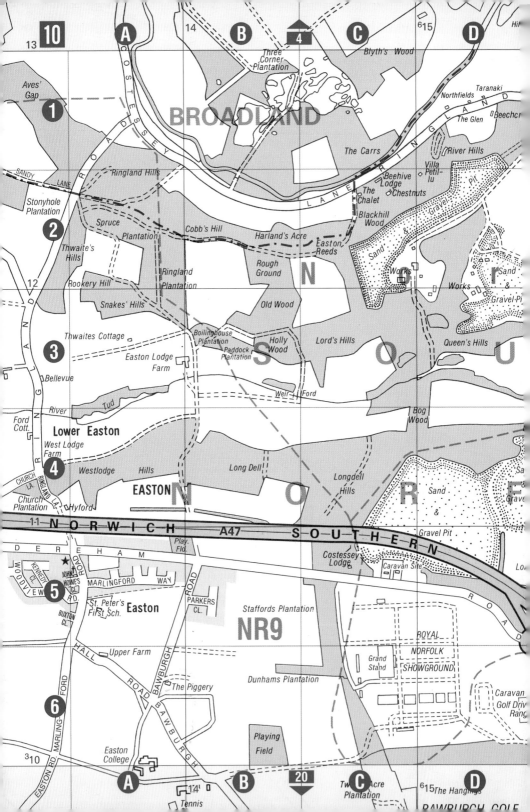

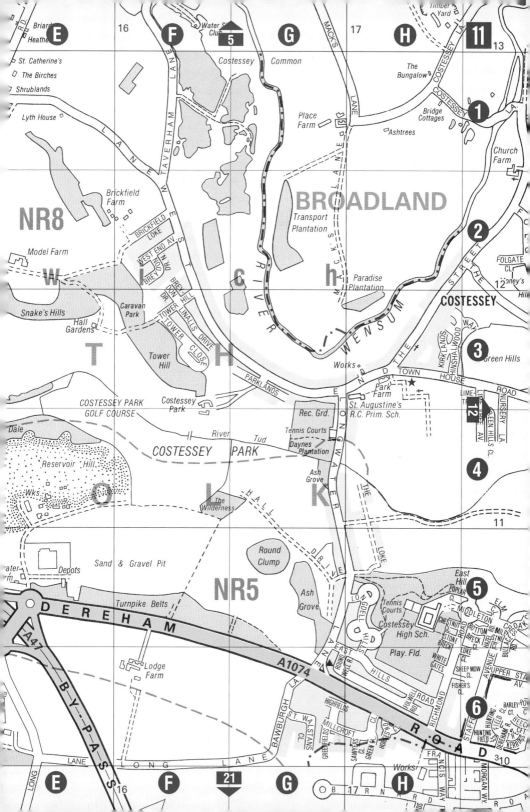

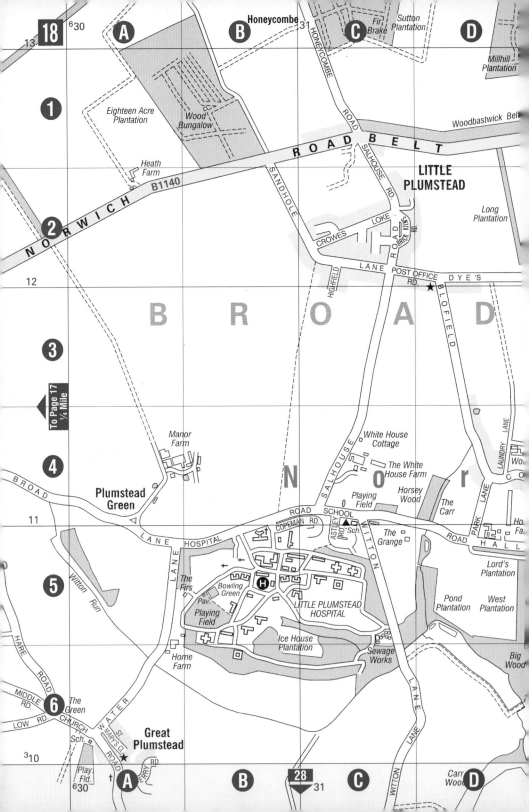

A

B **Honeycombe** 31

C Fir Brake · Sutton Plantation

D Millhill Plantation

1

Eighteen Acre Plantation

Wood Bungalow

Woodbastwick Belt

ROAD BELT

Heath Farm

NORWICH B1140

SANDHOLE ROAD

SALHOUSE RD.

CROWES LOKE

BRICK KILNS

ROAD

LITTLE PLUMSTEAD

Long Plantation

2
12

HIGHFIELD LANE

POST OFFICE RD.

DYE'S

BLOFIELD

B R O A D

3

To Page 17 ¼ Mile

Manor Farm

SALHOUSE ROAD

White House Cottage

The White House Farm

N Horsey Wood

O The Carr

r Wo

LAUNDRY LANE

PARK LANE

4
11

BROAD LANE

Plumstead Green

COPEMAN RD.

SCHOOL ROAD

ASTLEY RD.

Sch.

Playing Field

WITTON ROAD

The Grange

HALL ROAD

Ho Fa

Lord's Plantation

5

Witton Run

HOSPITAL LANE

The Firs

Bowling Green

Pav.

Playing Field

H

LITTLE PLUMSTEAD HOSPITAL

Pond Plantation

West Plantation

Ice House Plantation

Sewage Works

Big Wood

HARE ROAD

Home Farm

6
3 10

MIDDLE RD.

LOW RD.

CHURCH

Sch.

The Green

WATER

MARY'S ST.

COPY RD.

Great Plumstead

Play. Fld. 6 30

A

B

28 31

C

WITTON LANE

Carr Wood

D

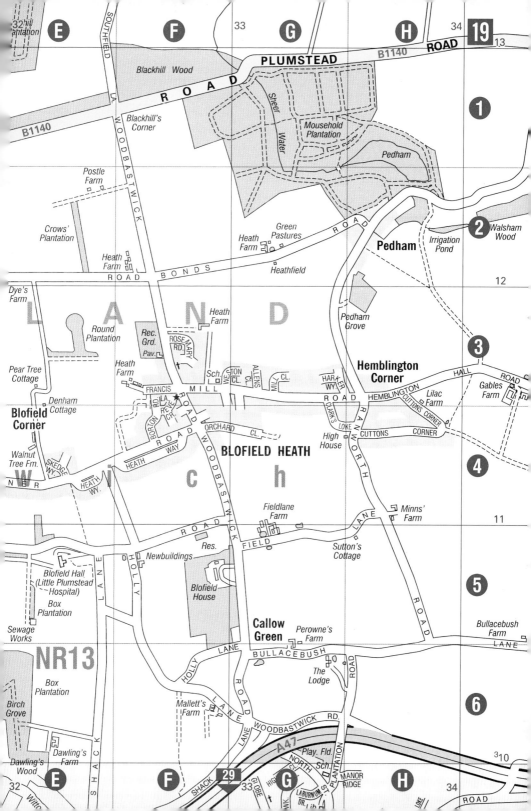

Map page — Blofield Heath / Plumstead area (NR13)

PLUMSTEAD ROAD · B1140

B1140

Blackhill Wood

Blackhill's Corner

ROAD

SOUTHFIELD LA

WOODBASTWICK

Sheer Water

Mousehold Plantation

Pedham

1

2 Walsham Wood

Irrigation Pond

Pedham

Postle Farm

Crows' Plantation

Heath Farm

ROAD

BONDS

Heath Farm

Green Pastures

Heathfield

12

Pedham Grove

Dye's Farm

L A N D

Round Plantation

Rec. Grd. Pav.

Heath Farm

ROSEMARY RD.

Sch.

WESTON CL.

ALLENS CL.

MILL CL.

Heath Farm

HARKER WY.

ROAD

Clark's LOKE

High House

Hemblington Corner

HEMBLINGTON

CUTTONS CORNER

Lilac Farm

HALL

ROAD

Gables Farm

3

RANWORTH

CUTTONS CORNER

Pear Tree Cottage

Denham Cottage

Blofield Corner

FRANCIS LA.

BORTON RD.

PEVE CR.

MILL

ROAD

ORCHARD

CL.

BLOFIELD HEATH

c

h

4

Walnut Tree Fm.

SKEDGE WY.

HEATH WY.

NWBR

HEATH WY.

WOODBASTWICK

ROAD

Fieldlane Farm

Res.

FIELD

LANE

Minns' Farm

Sutton's Cottage

11

Newbuildings

HOLLY

Blofield Hall (Little Plumstead Hospital)

Box Plantation

Sewage Works

NR13

Box Plantation

Birch Grove

Dawling's Wood

Dawling's Farm

SHACK LANE

HOLLY LANE

Res.

Blofield House

Callow Green

Perowne's Farm

BULLACEBUSH

The Lodge

ROAD

WOODBASTWICK

ROAD

5

Bullacebush Farm

LANE

6

Mallett's Farm

LANE

SHACK

A47

Play. Fld.

Sch.

PLANTATION

MANOR RIDGE

ROAD

3 10

GLOBE

NORTH ST.

HIGH ST.

LABURNUM DR. Lib.

WOODBASTWICK RD.

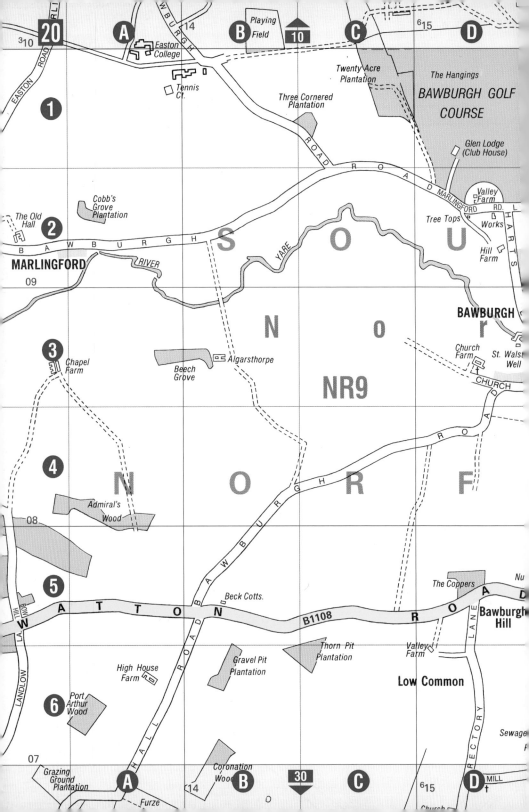

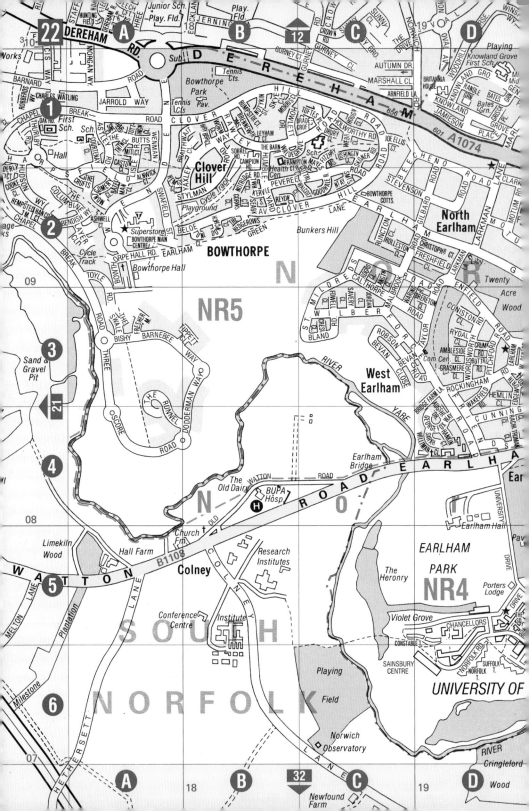

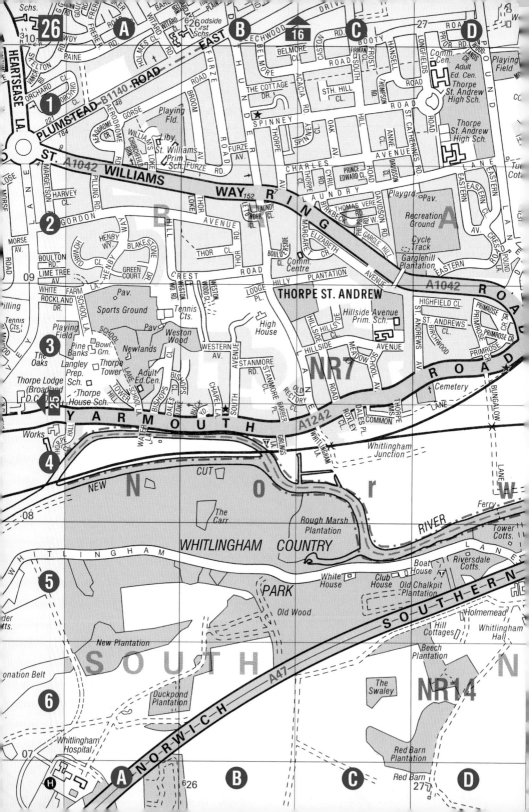

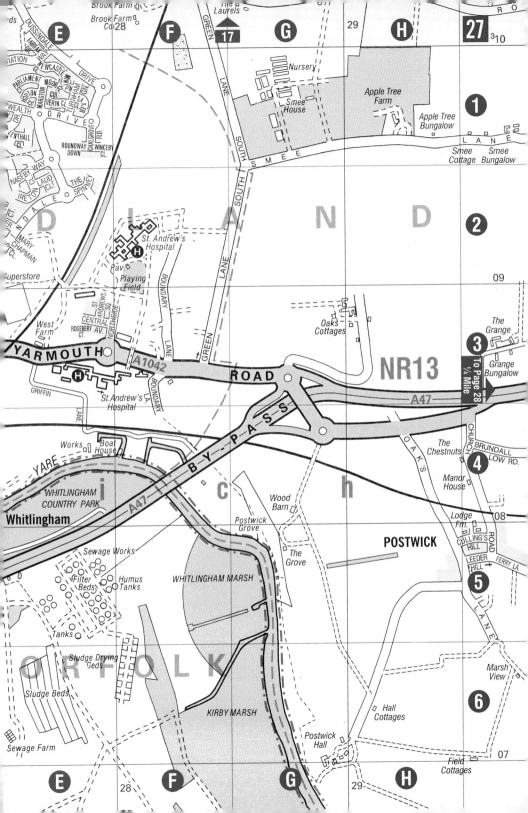

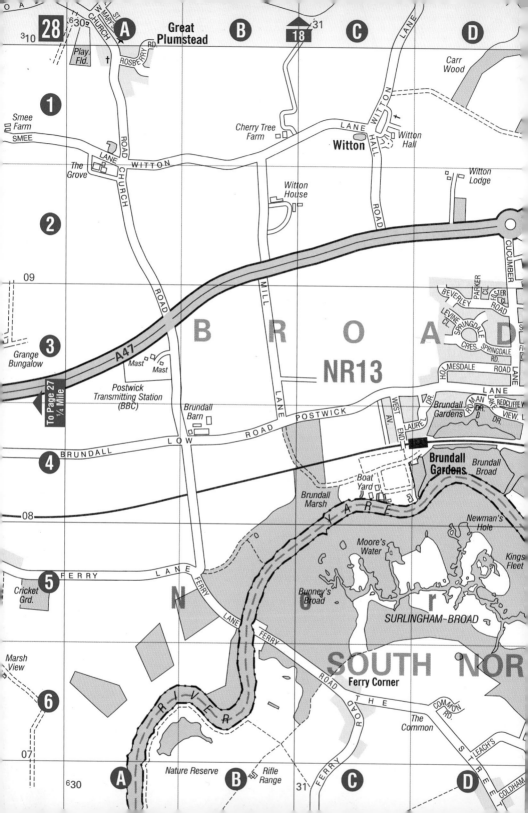

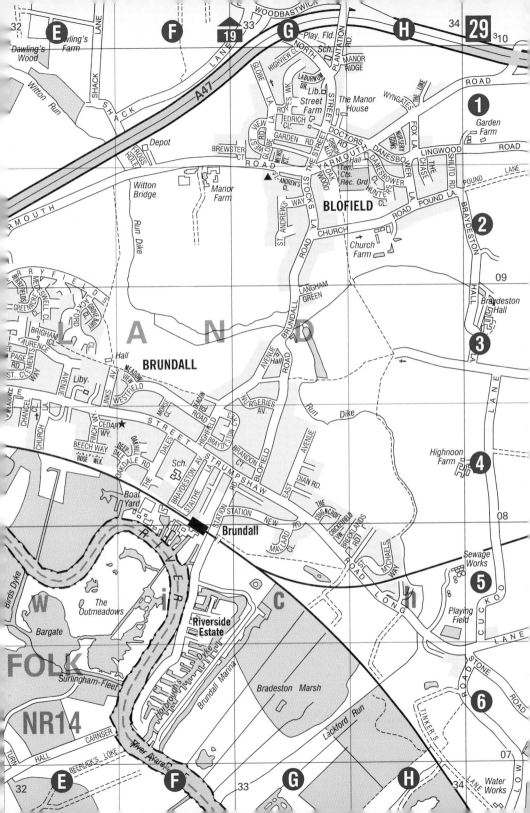

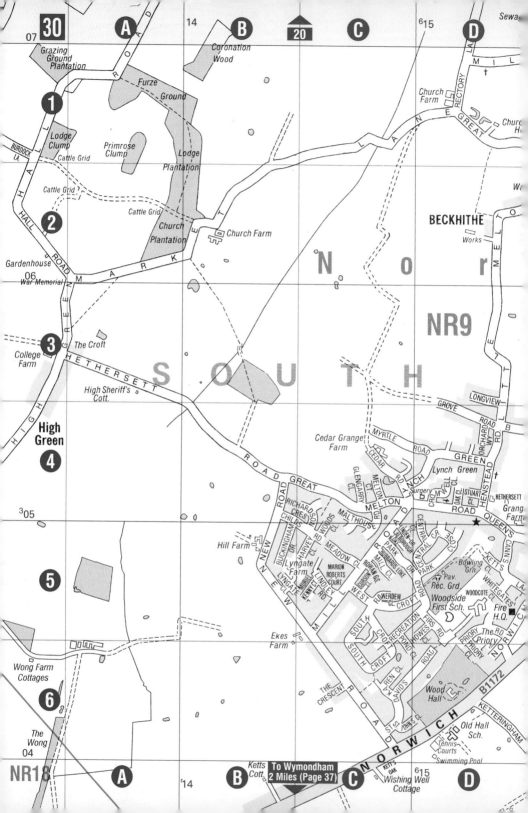

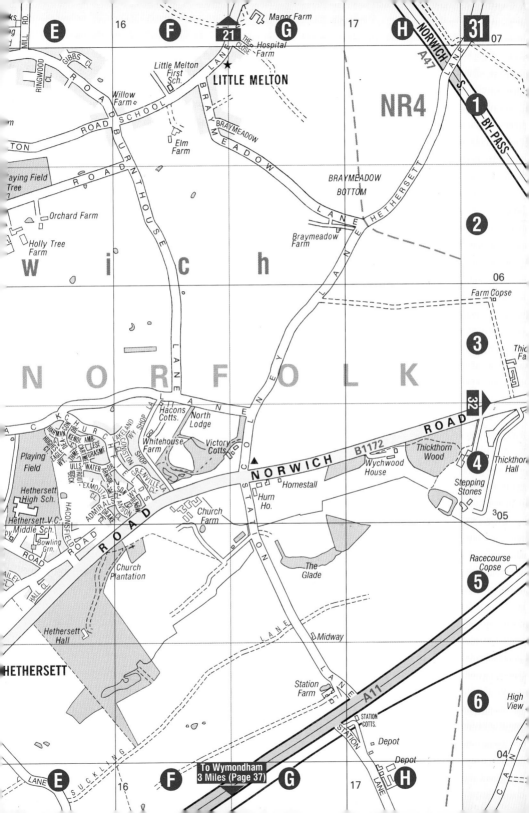

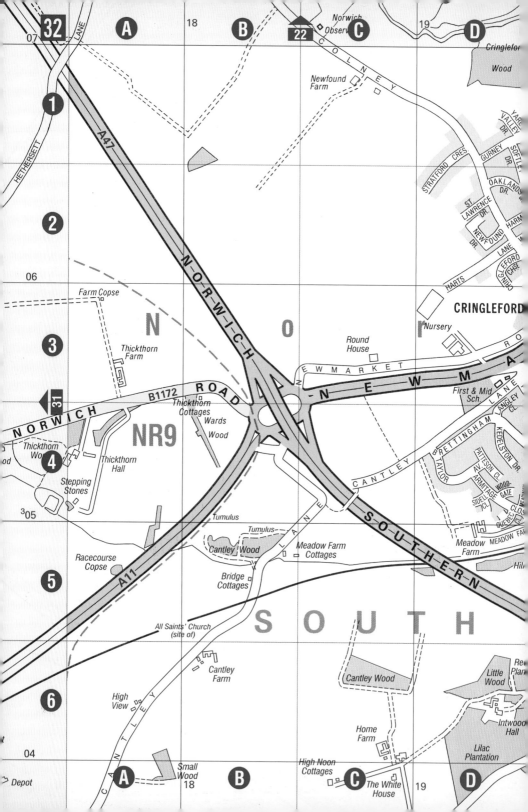

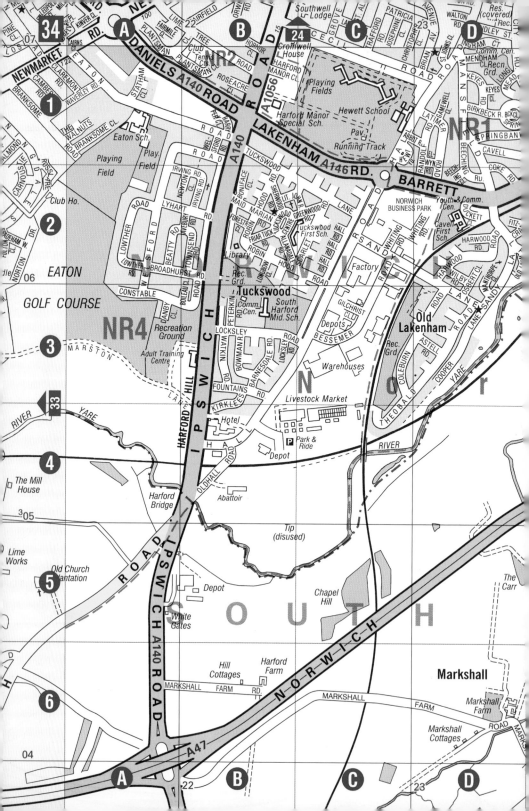

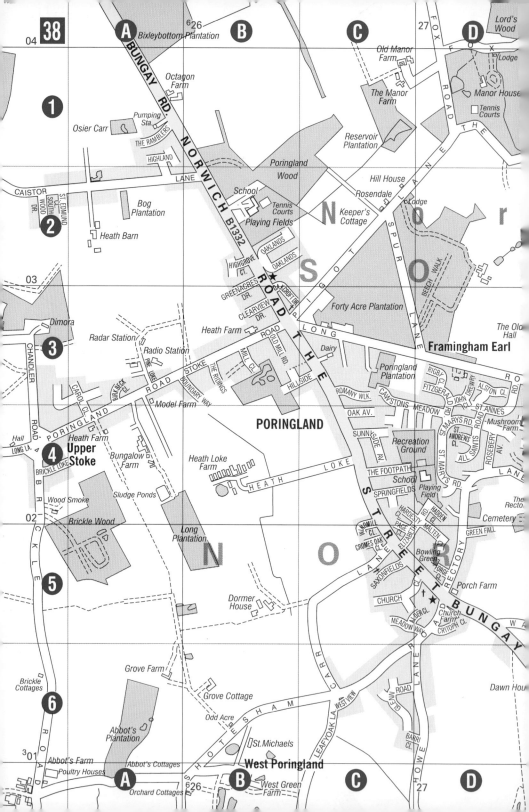

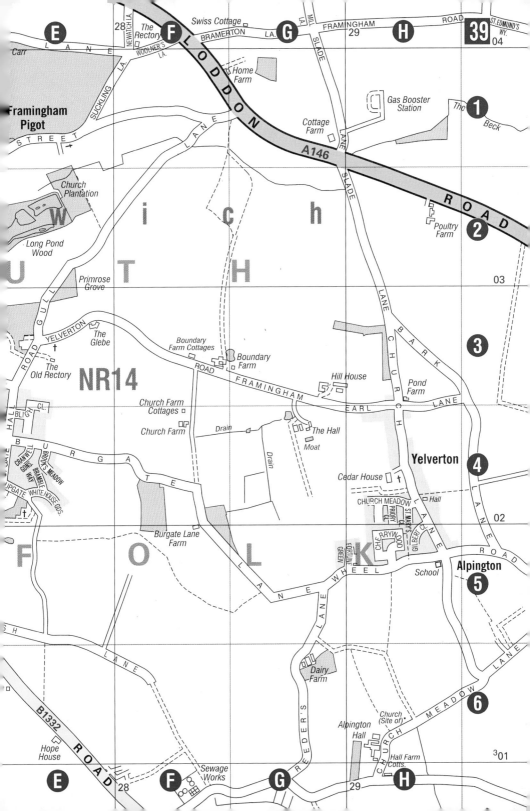

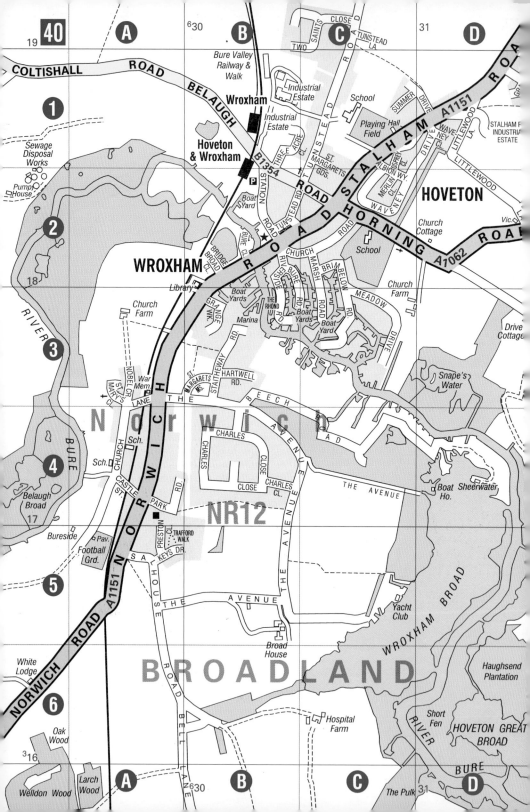

INDEX TO STREETS

HOW TO USE THIS INDEX

1. Each street name is followed by its Postal Locality, and then by its map reference; e.g. Abbey Clo. NR10 —3A **8** is in the Norwich 10 Postal District and is found in square 3A on page **8**. The page number being shown in bold type.
   A strict alphabetical order is followed in which Av., Rd., St. etc. (though abbreviated) are read in full and as part of the street name; e.g. Ashdown appears after Ash Clo. but before Ash Gro.

2. Streets and a selection of Subsidiary names not shown on the Maps, appear in this index in *Italics* with the thoroughfare to which it is connected shown in brackets; e.g. *Charles Wesley Ct. NR2 —3A* **24** *(off Belvoir St.)*

3. With the now general usage of Postcodes for addressing mail, it is not recommended that this index be used for such a purpose.

GENERAL ABBREVIATIONS

All: Alley	Chyd: Churchyard	Gdns: Gardens	Mans: Mansions	Sq: Square
App: Approach	Circ: Circle	Ga: Gate	Mkt: Market	Sta: Station
Arc: Arcade	Cir: Circus	Gt: Great	M: Mews	St: Street
Av: Avenue	Clo: Close	Grn: Green	Mt: Mount	Ter: Terrace
Bk: Back	Comn: Common	Gro: Grove	N: North	Up: Upper
Boulevd: Boulevard	Cotts: Cottages	Ho: House	Pal: Palace	Vs: Villas
Bri: Bridge	Ct: Court	Ind: Industrial	Pde: Parade	Wlk: Walk
B'way: Broadway	Cres: Crescent	Junct: Junction	Pk: Park	W: West
Bldgs: Buildings	Dri: Drive	La: Lane	Pas: Passage	Yd: Yard
Bus: Business	E: East	Lit: Little	Pl: Place	
Cen: Centre	Embkmt: Embankment	Lwr: Lower	Rd: Road	
Chu: Church	Est: Estate	Mnr: Manor	S: South	

INDEX TO STREETS

Abbey Clo. NR10 —3A **8**
Abbey Ct. NR1 —5E **25** (8E **3**)
Abbey La. NR1 —4E **25** (6E **3**)
Abbey Rd. NR10 —3A **8**
Abbot Clo. NR18 —3D **36**
Abbot Rd. NR1 —1C **34**
Aberdare Rd. NR1 —2G **25**
Abinger Way. NR4 —4H **33**
Acacia Rd. NR7 —1B **26**
Acland M. NR6 —3B **14**
Acres Way. NR8 —3H **5**
Adams Rd. NR7 —2F **15**
Addey Clo. NR6 —2E **15**
Adelaide St. NR2 —2A **24**
Admirals Way. NR4 —4E **31**
Aerodrome Cres. NR7 —1A **26**
Aerodrome Rd. NR7 —1A **26**
Agricultural Hall Plain. NR1
  —3D **24** (4D **2**)
Aitken Clo. NR2 —2G **15**
Alan Rd. NR1 —5E **25** (8E **3**)
Albany Rd. NR3 —1C **24**
Albemarle Rd. NR2 —6A **24**
Albert Pl. NR1 —3F **25**
Albert Ter. NR2 —4E **15**
Albion Dri. NR7 —4F **15**
Albion Way. NR12 —1C **40**
Alborough Loke. NR9 —5C **30**
Albury Wlk. NR4 —2G **33**
Alder Clo. NR14 —5D **38**
Alderson Pl. NR1 —8D **3**
Alder Way. NR8 —4H **5**
Aldryche Rd. NR1 —1G **25**
Aldwick Rd. NR4 —6G **33**
Alexander Ct. NR4 —6G **33**
Alexandra Rd. NR2 —6A **24**
Alford Gro. NR7 —4F **15**
Alfred Nicholls Ct. NR2 —5C **14**
Allandale Rd. NR4 —2B **34**
Allen Brooks Way. NR18
  —5D **36**
Allens Av. NR7 —3F **15**
Allen Clo. NR13 —3G **19**
Allens La. NR7 —3E **15**
Allerton Clo. NR7 —5D **24** (7C **3**)
Allerton Rd. NR7 —4G **15**
All Saints Grn. NR1
  —5D **24** (7C **3**)
All Saints Rd. NR1
  —4D **24** (6C **3**)
Almary Grn. NR1 —3D **2**
Alma Ter. NR3 —1C **24**
Alms La. NR3 —2B **2**
Alnwick Ct. NR5 —2A **22**
Alston Clo. NR14 —3D **38**
Alston Rd. NR6 —4F **13**
Alton Ga. NR7 —4F **15**
Ambleside. NR9 —4E **31**
Ambleside Clo. NR5 —1H **21**
Amderley Dri. NR4 —2G **33**
Amhirst Clo. NR3 —6E **15**
Ampthill St. NR2 —4B **24**
Amsterdam Way. NR6 —1H **13**
Anchor Clo. NR3 —2E **25** (1E **2**)

Anchor Quay. NR3 —3B **2**
Anchor St. NR3 —1E **25** (1E **2**)
Angela Clo. NR10 —1G **7**
Angela Cres. NR10 —1G **7**
Angela Rd. NR10 —1G **7**
Angel Rd. NR3 —5C **14**
Anglia Sq. NR3 —2D **24** (1C **2**)
Anmer Clo. NR3 —4E **15**
Anna Sewell Dri. NR6 —2D **14**
Anne Clo. NR7 —1C **26**
Annes Wlk. NR3 —1C **2**
Anson Clo. NR9 —4F **31**
Anson Rd. NR6 —1A **14**
Anthony Dri. NR3 —5E **15**
Antingham Rd. NR7 —6A **16**
Applegarth. NR18 —4C **36**
Applegarth Ct. NR18 —4C **36**
Appleyard Cres. NR3 —4H **13**
Apsley Ct. NR5 —3G **23**
Arcade St. NR2 —4D **24** (5C **3**)
Archer Clo. NR6 —1F **15**
Arden Gro. NR6 —6F **7**
Arderon Ct. NR2 —1H **23**
Ardney Rise. NR3 —4C **14**
Argyle St. NR1 —5E **25** (7E **3**)
Argyll Cres. NR8 —5G **5**
Arlington La. NR2 —5B **24**
Armes Cres. NR2 —1H **23**
Armes St. NR2 —1H **23**
Arminghall Clo. NR3 —4B **14**
Arminghall La. NR14 —4F **35**
Armitage Clo. NR4 —4D **32**
Arms Pk. Rd. NR6 —1A **14**
Armstrong Rd. NR7 —5B **16**
  (in two parts)
Arneside. NR9 —4E **31**
Arnfield La. NR5 —1C **22**
Arnold Miller Clo. NR4 —2B **34**
Arnold Miller Rd. NR1 —1E **35**
Arthurton Rd. NR7 —3F **9**
Arundel Ct. NR2 —8A **3**
Arundel Rd. NR18 —2D **36**
Ashbourne Ind. Est. NR6
  —3A **14**
Ashbourne Tower. NR7 —5A **16**
Ashby St. NR1 —5D **24** (7C **3**)
Ash Clo. NR18 —2E **37**
Ashdown. NR8 —4H **5**
Ash Gro. NR3 —5D **14**
Ashgrove. NR8 —3H **5**
Ashleigh Gdns. NR18 —2F **37**
Ashtree Rd. NR5 —5B **12**
Ashwell Ct. NR5 —2A **22**
Aspen Way. NR4 —3E **33**
Aspland Rd. NR1 —3E **25** (4F **2**)
Association Way. NR7 —1E **27**
Astell Rd. NR1 —1E **35**
Astley Rd. NR15 —1A **42**
Astley Rd. NR13 —5C **18**
Atkinson Clo. NR5 —1H **21**
Atmere Clo. NR4 —2G **33**
Atthill Rd. NR2 —2H **23**
Augustus Hare Dri. NR5
  —4D **22**
Aurania Av. NR1 —6C **24**
Auster Clo. NR6 —3B **14**

Autumn Dri. NR5 —1C **22**
Avebury Rd. NR4 —2B **34**
Avenue Rd. NR2 —4A **24**
Avenue Rd. NR18 —5D **36**
Avenues, The. NR2 —4H **23**
Avenue, The. NR12 —4B **40**
Avian Way. NR7 —5H **15**
Avonmouth Rd. NR3 —6B **14**
Aylesbury Clo. NR3 —5C **14**
Aylmer Tower. NR3 —5H **13**
Aylsham Cres. NR3 —4B **14**
Aylsham Rd. NR3 —4A **14**
Aylsham Way. NR3 —5B **14**
Ayton Rd. NR18 —5D **36**
Ayton Rd. Ind. Est. NR18
  —5E **37**

Back La. NR8 —4A **4**
Back La. NR8 —4D **30**
Back La. NR18 —4C **36**
Back of the Inns. NR2 —5C **3**
Back St. NR10 —3A **8**
Bacon Rd. NR2 —4G **23**
Bacton Rd. NR3 —5A **14**
Badgers Brook Rd. NR8 —3H **5**
Bagley Ct. NR2 —4B **2**
Bagleys Ct. NR2 —3C **24** (4B **2**)
Bailey Clo. NR9 —5E **31**
Bailey Ct. NR2 —2B **24**
Bainards Clo. NR3 —1C **26**
Baker's La. NR3 —1C **24**
Balderston Ct. NR3
  —3D **24** (2C **2**)
Baldric Rd. NR8 —4G **5**
Balfour St. NR3 —1C **24**
Banister Way. NR18 —3B **36**
Bank Plain. NR2 —3D **24** (4C **2**)
Bank St. NR2 —3D **24** (4D **2**)
Barber Pl. NR7 —4B **26**
Barberry Clo. NR8 —3E **5**
Barclay Grn. NR7 —6B **16**
Barclay Rd. NR7 —6A **16**
Bardolph Rd. NR3 —2D **24** (1D **2**)
Barker's La. NR7 —2F **15**
Barker St. NR2 —1B **24**
Barker Way. NR7 —4E **17**
Bark La. NR14 —3H **39**
Barley Ct. NR5 —6A **12**
Barnard Rd. NR5 —1H **21**
Barnards Yd. NR3 —3B **2**
Barnes Clo. NR7 —5A **16**
Barnesdale Rd.,NR4 —3B **34**
Barnham Broom Rd. NR18
  —1B **36**
Barnham Clo. NR5 —2H **21**
Barn Rd. NR2 —3B **24** (3A **2**)
Barn, The. NR5 —2B **22**
Barrack Rd. NR1 —2G **25**
Barrack St. NR3 —2D **24** (1D **2**)
Barrett-Lennard Rd. NR10
  —1F **7**
Barrett Rd. NR1 —2C **34**
Barri Clo. NR14 —6C **38**
Barrow Clo. NR3 —6G **13**
Barwells Ct. NR2 —6B **3**

Bassingham Rd. NR3 —5A **14**
Bateman Clo. NR5 —2A **22**
Bates Grn. NR5 —1D **22**
Bathurst Rd. NR2 —4A **24**
Bawburgh La. NR5 —6G **11**
Bawburgh Rd. NR9 —5B **20**
  (Bawburgh)
Bawburgh Rd. NR9 —2A **20**
  (Marlingford)
Baxter Ct. NR3 —4A **14**
Beachcroft. NR7 —5E **15**
Beaconsfield Rd. NR3 —1D **24**
Beatrice Rd. NR1 —3F **25**
Beatty Rd. NR4 —2A **34**
Beaumont Pl. NR2 —5B **24**
Beaumont Rd. NR5 —5C **12**
Becketswell Rd. NR18 —5C **36**
Becketts Ct. NR18 —2C **36**
Beckham Pl. NR3
  —2D **24** (1C **2**)
Beck La. NR10 —1B **8**
Becks Fur. NR8 —3H **5**
Bedding La. NR3
  —2D **24** (2D **2**)
Bedford St. NR2 —3D **24** (4C **2**)
Beech Av. NR8 —4D **4**
Beechbank. NR2 —5A **24**
Beechbank Ct. NR2 —5A **24**
Beechbank Dri. NR13 —4E **17**
Beech Clo. NR18 —2E **37**
Beech Croft. NR5 —6A **12**
Beech Dri. NR1 —1F **25**
Beech Dri. NR6 —3B **14**
Beecheno Rd. NR5 —2C **22**
Beeches Clo. NR6 —3D **14**
Beeching Clo. NR1 —2D **34**
Beeching Rd. NR1 —1D **34**
Beechlands. NR8 —4E **5**
Beech Rd. NR2 —5A **24**
Beech Rd. NR12 —3B **40**
Beech Wlk. NR4 —5F **33**
Beech Wlk. NR14 —3D **38**
Beech Way. NR13 —4E **29**
Beechwood Dri. NR7 —6B **16**
Beechwoods. NR6 —2C **14**
Beerlick's Loke. NR14 —6E **29**
Beeston La. NR12 & NR13
  —5F **9**
Bek Clo. NR4 —1F **33**
Belaugh Rd. NR12 —1B **40**
Bell Clo. NR6 —1G **13**
Bell Clo. NR8 —5H **5**
Bellingham Ct. NR3 —6D **14**
Bell La. NR12 —6A **40**
Bellomonte Cres. NR8 —5A **6**
Bell Rd. NR3 —6D **14**
Bellrope Clo. NR18 —3E **37**
Bellrope La. NR18 —3E **37**
Bellville Cres. NR1
  —5E **25** (8E **3**)
Belmore Clo. NR7 —1B **26**
Belmore Rd. NR7 —1B **26**
Beloe Av. NR5 —2B **22**
Belsize Rd. NR1 —2G **25**
Belt Rd. NR13 —1C **18**
Belvedere Pl. NR4 —6A **24**

Belvoir St. NR2 —3A **24**
Benbow Clo. NR9 —4F **31**
Bendish Way. NR5 —2H **21**
Bensley Rd. NR2 —4H **23**
Bentley Way. NR6 —3B **14**
Berkley Clo. NR6 —2H **13**
Bernard Rd. NR13 —2G **17**
Berners Clo. NR3 —6A **14**
Berners St. NR3 —6B **14**
Bernham Rd. NR6 —1F **13**
Berrington Rd. NR6 —1G **13**
Berryfields. NR13 —2E **29**
Ber St. NR1 —4D **24** (6C **3**)
Bertie Rd. NR3 —6B **14**
Bessemer Rd. NR4 —3C **34**
Bethel St. NR2 —3C **24** (4A **2**)
Bevan Clo. NR5 —3C **22**
Beverley Clo. NR3 —5F **23**
Beverley Rd. NR5 —2F **23**
Beverley Rd. NR13 —3D **28**
Beverley Way. NR8 —5A **6**
Bewfield Rd. NR5 —1H **21**
Bewit Rd. NR7 —3A **16**
Bidewell Clo. NR8 —6C **6**
Bignold Rd. NR3 —5H **13**
Billing Clo. NR6 —1E **15**
Binyon Gdns. NR8 —5G **5**
Birch Ct. NR7 —3A **16**
Birchwood. NR7 —3D **26**
Birkbeck Clo. NR1 —1D **34**
Birkbeck Clo. NR14 —3A **38**
Birkbeck Rd. NR1 —1D **34**
Birkbeck Way. NR7 —2C **26**
Birkdale. NR4 —1H **33**
Bishop Bri. Rd. NR1 —2F **25**
Bishopgate. NR3 & NR1
  —2E **25** (2E **2**)
Bishop Pelham Ct. NR4 —6G **33**
Bishop Rise. NR8 —3H **5**
Bishops Clo. NR7 —3A **26**
Bishy Barnebee Way. NR5
  —3A **22**
Bixley Clo. NR5 —3E **23**
Blackberry Ct. NR6 —5G **13**
Blackfriars St. NR3
  —2D **24** (1D **2**)
Blackhorse La. NR3 —5E **15**
Blackhorse Opening. NR3
  —5E **15**
Blackhorse St. NR2 —2B **24**
Blacksmiths Way. NR6 —2D **14**
Blackthorn Clo. NR6 —2C **14**
Blackwell Av. NR7 —5F **15**
Blakeney Clo. NR4 —1F **33**
Blakes St. NR3 —4E **15**
Blakestone Dri. NR7 —2A **26**
Bland Rd. NR5 —3C **22**
Blenheim Clo. NR7 —2G **15**
Blenheim Cres. NR7 —3G **15**
Blenheim Rd. NR7 —2G **15**
Blickling Ct. NR1 —4E **2**
Blickling Rd. NR6 —2B **14**
Bligh Clo. NR14 —4E **39**
Blind La. NR10 —3A **8**
Blithe Meadow Ct. NR7 —4H **15**

A-Z Norwich 41

Blithe-Meadow Dri. NR7 —4H **15**
Blithewood Gdns. NR7 —4H **15**
Blofield Corner Rd. NR13 —3D **18**
Blofield Rd. NR13 —4G **29**
Blomefield Rd. NR3 —5A **14**
Bluebell Cres. NR4 —1E **33**
Bluebell Rd. NR4 —4E **23**
Blue Boar La. NR7 —2H **15**
Blyth Rd. NR3 —5C **14**
Boardman Clo. NR3 —4C **14**
Boilleau Clo. NR4 —3A **34**
Bolingbroke Rd. NR3 —4A **14**
Bonds Rd. NR13 —2F **19**
Bond St. NR2 —2H **23**
Bone Rd. NR8 —5C **6**
Boniface Clo. NR4 —2B **34**
Booty Rd. NR7 —6C **16**
Borrowdale Dri. NR1 —1G **25**
Borton Rd. NR13 —4F **19**
Boston St. NR3 —5C **14**
Boswell's Yd. NR3 —2C **2**
Botolph St. NR3 —2C **24** (1B **2**)
Botolph Way. NR3 —1C **2**
Bottom Breck Clo. NR5 —5A **12**
Boulderside Clo. NR7 —2B **26**
Boulevard, The. NR13 —4F **17**
Boulton Rd. NR7 —2H **25**
Boulton St. NR1 —4D **24** (5D **3**)
Boundary Av. NR6 —4H **13**
Boundary La. NR7 —2F **27**
Boundary Rd. NR6 & NR3 (in two parts) —4G **13**
Boundary Way. NR14 —3B **38**
Bowers Av. NR3 —4H **13**
Bowers Clo. NR3 —5H **13**
Bow Hill. NR9 —5A **20**
Bowling Grn. Clo. NR10 —2G **9**
Bowman Rd. NR4 —3B **34**
Bowthorpe Cotts. NR5 —2C **22**
Bowthorpe Hall Rd. NR5 —2A **22**
Bowthorpe Main Cen. NR5 —2A **22**
Bowthorpe Rd. NR2 —3G **23**
Bowthorpe Rd. NR5 —3E **23**
Brabazon Rd. NR6 —2A **14**
Bracey Av. NR6 —2E **15**
Bracken Av. NR6 —3H **13**
Bracondale. NR1 —5E **25** (8E **3**)
Bracondale Ct. NR1 —6E **25**
Bracondale Grn. NR1 —5E **25** (8E **3**)
Brade Croft. NR5 —1C **22**
Bradeham Way. NR4 —2H **33**
Bradshaw Rd. NR8 —6D **6**
Braeford Clo. NR6 —5F **13**
Braithwait Clo. NR5 —1B **22**
Bramble Av. NR6 —2H **13**
Bramble Clo. NR8 —3H **5**
Brambles Clo. NR10 —3F **9**
Bramble Way. NR14 —4E **39**
Bramerton La. NR14 —1F **39**
Bramfield Clo. NR2 —2H **23**
Brampton Ct. NR5 —1B **22**
Brandon Clo. NR6 —3F **13**
Brandon Ct. NR13 —4G **29**
Branford Rd. NR3 —6D **14**
Branksome Clo. NR4 —1A **34**
Branksome Rd. NR4 —1H **33**
Brasier Rd. NR3 —4A **14**
Braydeston Av. NR13 —4F **29**
Braydeston Cres. NR13 —4F **29**
Braydeston Hall La. NR13 —2H **29**
Brayfield Way. NR6 —1E **15**
Braymeadow. NR9 —1F **31**
Braymeadow La. NR9 —1F **31**
Brazen Ga. NR1 —5C **24** (7B **3**)
Brech Farm Clo. NR8 —3F **5**
Breck Farm Clo. NR8 —3F **5**
Breck Farm La. NR8 —3F **5**
Breckland Rd. NR5 —6B **12**
Brecklands Rd. NR13 —5G **29**
Breck Rd. NR7 —5B **16**
Brennewater M. NR5 —1B **22**
Brentwood. NR4 —2G **33**
Brereton Clo. NR5 —3D **22**
Brettingham Av. NR4 —4D **32**
Brewers Ct. NR3 —2E **25** (1E **2**) (in two parts)
Brewery La. NR18 —5D **36**
Brewster Ct. NR13 —1F **29**
Breydon Dri. NR8 —3F **11**
Breydon Dri. N. NR8 —2F **11**
Breydon Rd. NR7 —3E **15**
Brian Av. NR1 —6C **24**
Briar Ct. NR5 —2G **23**
Brickfield Loke. NR8 —2F **11**
Brick Kilns Rd. NR13 —2C **18**
Brickle Loke. NR14 —4A **38**
Brickle Rd. NR14 —4A **38**
Bridewell All. NR2 —4C **2**
Bridewell St. NR18 —5D **36**
Bridge Broad Clo. NR12 —2B **40**
Bridge Ct. NR3 —2D **24** (2C **2**)
Bridge Farm La. NR5 —3D **22**
Bridge Ind. Est. NR18 —6D **36**
Bridle La. NR4 —6G **33**
Brigg St. NR2 —4C **24** (5B **3**)
Brigham Clo. NR13 —3E **29**
Brightwell Rd. NR3 —4C **14**
Brightys Opening. NR2 —2H **23**
Brimbelow Rd. NR12 —2C **40**
Bristol Ter. NR2 —4C **24** (6A **3**)
Britannia Ho. NR5 —1D **22**
Britannia Rd. NR1 —1F **25**
Britonway. NR18 —5C **36**
Broadhurst Rd. NR4 —2A **34**
Broadland Dri. NR7 —4E **17**
Broadland Dri. NR13 —4E **17**
Broad La. NR13 —3G **17**
Broadmead Grn. NR13 —4F **17**
Broad View. NR7 —4E **17**
Brockwell Ct. NR3 —5E **15**
Bronde Clo. NR6 —1D **14**
Brooke Pl. NR1 —4D **24** (6C **3**)
Brooks Meadow. NR14 —4E **39**
Brooks Rd. NR10 —2G **7**
Broom Av. NR6 —2H **13**
Broom Av. NR7 —1B **26**
Broom Clo. NR1 —6E **25**
Browick Rd. NR18 —5D **36**
Browne St. NR2 —2A **24**
Brundall Low Rd. NR13 —4H **27**
Brundall Rd. NR13 —3G **29**
Brunswick Rd. NR2 & NR1 —5C **24**
Bryony Clo. NR6 —2C **14**
Buckingham Dri. NR9 —5B **30**
Buckingham Rd. NR4 —6G **23**
Buckland Rise. NR4 —3G **33**
Buckthorn Clo. NR8 —3E **5**
Buck Yd. NR7 —4B **26**
Bullacebush La. NR13 —6G **19**
Bullace Rd. NR5 —5A **12**
Bullard Rd. NR3 —4B **14**
Bull Clo. NR3 —2D **24** (1D **2**)
Bull Clo. Rd. NR3 (in two parts) —1D **24** (1D **2**)
Bull La. NR1 —5C **24** (7B **3**)
Bulmer Rd. NR3 —5H **13**
Bumpstede Ct. NR5 —1B **22**
Bungalow La. NR7 —3D **26**
Bungay Rd. NR14 —2H **35** (Arminghall)
Bungay Rd. NR14 —5D **38** (Poringland)
Bunnett Sq. NR4 —4G **23**
Burdock La. NR9 —1A **30**
Bure Clo. NR12 —2B **40**
Bure Rd. NR12 —2B **40**
Burgate La. NR14 —4E **39**
Burges Rd. NR3 —5A **14**
Burhill Clo. NR4 —3H **33**
Burleigh Tower. NR7 —5A **16**
Burma Rd. NR6 —2E **15**
Burnet Rd. NR3 —5G **13**
Burnthouse La. NR9 —1F **31**
Burton Clo. NR6 —2B **14**
Burton Dri. NR13 —1G **17**
Burton Rd. NR6 —2B **14**
Bury St. NR2 —5A **24**
Bush Rd. NR6 —6G **7**
Bussey Rd. NR6 —3C **14**
Buttermere Rd. NR5 —3D **22**
Butts, The. NR5 —1A **22**
Buxton Clo. NR9 —5A **10**
Buxton Rd. NR3 —1C **24**
Buxton Rd. NR12 & NR10 —6E **9**
Byfield Ct. NR3 —6B **14**
Byron Rd. NR8 —5G **5**
Cadge Clo. NR5 —2E **23**
Cadge Rd. NR5 —3E **23** (in two parts)
Caernarvon Rd. NR2 —3A **24**
Cairns Ct. NR4 —6A **24**
Caistor La. NR14 —6E **35** (Caistor St Edmund)
Caistor La. NR14 —2A **38** (Poringland)
Caledonian Way. NR6 —3B **14**
Caley Clo. NR3 —5G **13**
Calthorpe Rd. NR5 —2C **22**
Calvert St. NR3 —2D **24** (2C **2**)
Camberley Rd. NR4 —1H **33**
Camborne Clo. NR5 —6D **12**
Cambridge St. NR2 —5B **24**
Cameron Grn. NR8 —5H **5**
Camp Gro. NR1 —3F **25**
Campion Ho. NR5 —1B **22**
Camp Rd. NR8 —4F **5**
Cannell Grn. NR3 —2E **25** (1F **2**)
Cannerby La. NR7 —3G **15**
Cann's La. NR9 —5D **30**
Canterbury Pl. NR2 —2B **24**
Cantley La. NR4 —6A **32**
Capps Rd. NR3 —6D **14**
Cardiff Rd. NR2 —4A **24**
Cardigan Pl. NR2 —2B **24**
Carleton Clo. NR7 —4G **15**
Carleton Clo. NR18 —2D **36**
Carleton Rd. NR7 —4G **15**
Carlton Gdns. NR1 —7C **3**
Carlyle Rd. NR1 —6E **25**
Carnoustie. NR4 —2H **33**
Carol Clo. NR14 —3A **38**
Caroline Ct. NR4 —5G **23**
Carr La. NR14 —6C **38**
Carrow Hill. NR1 —5E **25** (8E **3**)
Carrow Rd. NR1 —5E **25** (8F **3**) (in three parts)
Carr's Hill Clo. NR8 —3B **12**
Carshalton Rd. NR1 —6E **25**
Carterford Dri. NR3 —4D **14**
Carter Rd. NR8 —5C **6**
Cartmel. NR9 —4E **31**
Castle Hill. NR1 —4D **24** (5C **3**)
Castle Mall. NR1 —4D **24** (5C **3**)
Castle Meadow. NR1 —4D **24** (5C **3**)
Castle Rise. NR8 —2H **5**
Castle St. NR2 —3D **24** (5C **3**)
Castle St. NR12 —4A **40**
Castleton Clo. NR5 —1A **22**
Caston Rd. NR7 —1C **26**
Cathedral St. NR1 —3E **25** (4E **2**)
Catherine Wheel Opening. NR3 —1C **24**
Cator Rd. NR8 —4A **6**
Cattle Mkt. St. NR1 —4D **24** (5D **3**)
Catton Chase. NR6 —2C **14**
Catton Ct. NR6 —1D **14**
Catton Gro. Rd. NR3 —4C **14**
Catton View Ct. NR3 —4C **14**
Causeway Clo. NR2 —2B **24**
Cavalier Clo. NR7 —2E **27**
Cavalry Ride. NR3 —1F **2**
Cavell Rd. NR1 —1D **34**
Cavendish Ct. NR1 —3E **25** (4F **2**)
Cavendish Ho. NR1 —3E **25** (4F **2**)
Cavick Cotts. NR18 —5B **36**
Cavick Rd. NR18 —5B **36**
Cawstons Meadow. NR14 —3C **38**
Cecil Gowing Ct. NR7 —3G **15**
Cecil Rd. NR1 —6B **24**
Cedar Av. NR10 —1G **9**
Cedar Ct. NR18 —2E **37**
Cedar Rd. NR1 —4F **25**
Cedar Rd. NR9 —4C **30**
Cedars, The. NR2 —5A **24**
Cedar Way. NR13 —4E **29**
Cemetery La. NR18 —5C **36**
Central Av. NR7 —3E **27**
Central Clo. NR9 —5D **30**
Central Cres. NR9 —5C **30**
Cere Rd. NR7 —3H **15**
Chalfont Wlk. NR4 —1F **33**
Chalgrove Field. NR7 —1E **27**
Chalk Hill Rd. NR1 —3E **25** (4F **2**)
Chamberlin Clo. NR3 —5C **14**
Chamberlin Rd. NR3 —6C **14**
Chambers Rd. NR3 —4A **14**
Chancel Clo. NR13 —4E **29**
Chancellors Dri. NR4 —6D **22**
Chandler Rd. NR14 —3A **38**
Chandler's Clo. NR18 —5C **36**
Chandlers Ct. NR4 —3G **33**
Chandler's Hill. NR18 —5C **36**
Chantry Rd. NR2 —4C **24** (5A **3**)
Chantry, The. NR2 —4C **24** (5B **3**)
Chapel All. NR1 —8D **3**
Chapel Break Rd. NR5 —1H **21**
Chapel Ct. NR6 —2G **13**
Chapel Field E. NR2 —4C **24** (6A **3**)
Chapel Field N. NR2 —4C **24** (5A **3**)
Chapel Field Rd. NR2 —4B **24**
Chapel La. NR7 —3B **26**
Chapel La. NR18 —2A **36**
Chapel Loke. NR1 —5D **24** (7C **3**)
Chapel Rd. NR5 —5B **12**
Charing Cross. NR2 —3C **24** (3B **2**)
Charles Av. NR7 —2B **26**
Charles Clo. NR12 —4B **40**
Charles Jewson Ct. NR3 —5A **14**
Charles Sq. NR2 —3B **24**
Charles Watling Way. NR5 —1H **21**
*Charles Wesley Ct. NR2 —3A **24** (off Belvoir St.)*
Charlton Rd. NR3 —2D **24** (1D **2**)
Chartwell Ct. NR7 —4E **15**
Chartwell Rd. NR6 & NR7 —4C **14**
Chase CLo. NR6 —2C **14**
Chase, The. NR13 —2H **29**
Chatham St. NR3 —2C **24** (1A **2**)
Chenery Dri. NR7 —2H **15**
Cherry Clo. NR1 —6D **24**
Cherrywood. NR14 —5H **39**
Chester Pl. NR2 —3B **24**
Chester St. NR2 —5B **24**
Chestnut Av. NR10 —1G **9**
Chestnut Clo. NR5 —5H **11**
Chestnut Ct. NR2 —4A **2**
Chestnut Hill. NR4 —2F **33**
Chestnuts. NR18 —3C **36**
Cheyham Mt. NR4 —2G **33**
Childs Rd. NR9 —4B **30**
Childs Ter. NR9 —3E **21**
Chipperfield Rd. NR7 —6A **16**
Chittock Clo. NR10 —3G **9**
Choseley Ct. NR18 —4D **36**
Christchurch Ct. NR2 —6A **24**
Christchurch Rd. NR2 —4H **23**
Christine Rd. NR10 —3G **9**
Christopher Clo. NR1 —6D **24**
Christopher Ct. NR5 —2D **22**
Church All. NR13 —1G **29**
Church Av. NR2 —6A **24**
Church Av. E. NR2 —6A **24**
Church Clo. NR2 —1A **24**
Church Clo. NR14 —6H **35** (Arminghall)
Church Clo. NR14 —5C **38** (Poringland)
Churchfield. NR4 —3E **33**
Churchfield Grn. NR7 —1A **26**
Churchfields. NR9 —4E **31**
Church Grn. NR7 —2G **15**
Churchill Rd. NR3 —1D **24**
Church La. NR4 —2F **33**
Church La. NR7 & NR12 —2G **15**
Church La. NR9 —4A **10**
Church La. NR10 —2D **8**
Church La. NR12 —4A **40**
Church La. NR13 —4E **29**
Church La. NR14 —3H **39**
Churchman Rd. NR7 —5H **15**
Church Meadow. NR14 —4H **39**
Church Meadow La. NR14 —6H **39**
Church Rd. NR12 —2B **40**
Church Rd. NR13 —2G **29** (Blofield)
Church Rd. NR13 —6A **18** (Great Plumstead)
Church Rd. NR13 —4H **27** (Postwick)
Church St. NR6 —2D **14**
Church St. NR9 —3D **20**
Church St. NR10 —2E **7** (Horsford)
Church St. NR10 —2A **8** (Horsham St Faith)
Church St. NR18 —4C **36**
Church View Clo. NR7 —2G **15**
Church View Ct. NR7 —2G **15**
Churston Clo. NR1 —6E **25**
Cintra Rd. NR1 —3G **25**
Cirrus Way. NR7 —5H **15**
City Rd. NR1 —1D **34**
City View Rd. NR6 —3H **13**
Civic Gdns. NR3 —4H **13**
Clabon First Clo. NR3 —4D **14**
Clabon Rd. NR3 —5E **15**
Clabon Second Clo. NR3 —4E **15**
Clabon Third Clo. NR3 —4E **15**
Clancy Rd. NR7 —6H **15**
Clare Clo. NR3 —6D **14**
Claremont Rd. NR4 —1H **33**
Clarence Rd. NR1 —4F **25**
Clarendon Rd. NR2 —4B **24**
Clarendon Steps. NR2 —4A **24**
Clarke Rd. NR3 —1D **24**
Clark's Loke. NR13 —4G **19**
Clarkson Rd. NR5 —2D **22**
Clearview Dri. NR14 —3B **38**
Clement Ct. NR2 —4C **2**
Cleveland Rd. NR2 —4B **24**
Clifton Clo. NR2 —2B **24**
Clifton Rd. NR18 —2D **36**
Clifton St. NR2 —2A **24**
Close, The. NR1 —3E **25** (3F **2**)
Close, The. NR9 —6G **21**
Clovelly Dri. NR6 —5F **13**
Clover Ct. NR6 —4E **15**
Clover Hill Rd. NR5 —1B **22**
Clover Rd. NR7 —3E **15**
Coach & Horses Row. NR2 —4C **24** (6A **3**)
Coach Ho. Ct. NR4 —6H **23**
Coachmans Ct. NR7 —3E **15**
Coach M. NR4 —6G **33**
Cobholm Way. NR7 —5H **15**
Coburg St. NR2 —4C **24** (6B **3**)
Cock St. NR18 —4C **36**
Coigncroft, The. NR13 —4G **29**
Coke Rd. NR1 —1D **34**
Coldershaw Rd. NR6 —3A **14**
Coldham Hall Carnser. NR14 —6D **28**
Coleburn Rd. NR1 —3C **34**
Colegate. NR3 —3C **24** (3B **2**) (in two parts)
Coleridge Clo. NR8 —5G **5**
Colindeep La. NR7 —3F **15**
Colkett Dri. NR6 —3D **14**
College La. NR4 —6G **33**
College Rd. NR2 —4H **23**
Collins Ct. NR3 —5C **14**
Colls Rd. NR7 —6A **16**
Colls Wlk. NR7 —6A **16**
Colman Rd. NR4 —4G **23**
Colney Dri. NR4 —3E **33**
Colney La. NR4 —5B **22**
Colney La. NR9 —4G **31**
Coltishall La. NR10 —2A **8**
Coltishall Rd. NR12 —1A **40**
Columbine, The. NR5 —2H **21**
Common La. NR7 —3C **26**
Common Rd. NR14 —6D **28**
Commonwealth Way. NR7 —1E **27**
Compass Tower. NR7 —5A **16**
Concorde Rd. NR6 —3B **14**
Conesford Dri. NR1 —6E **25**
Coniston Clo. NR5 —3D **22**
Coniston Clo. NR9 —4F **31**
Connaught Rd. NR2 —3A **24**
Constable Rd. NR4 —3A **34**
Constable Ter. NR4 —5C **22**
Constitution Hill. NR3 & NR6 —6D **14**
Constitution Opening. NR3 —5D **14**
Convent Rd. NR2 —4B **24**
Conyers. NR18 —2D **36**
Cooke Clo. NR5 —2H **21**
Cooper La. NR1 —3D **34**
Coopers Clo. NR8 —2H **5**
Copeman Rd. NR13 —5B **18**
Copeman St. NR2 —3B **24**
Coppice Av. NR6 —2F **13**
Corbet Av. NR7 —5F **15**
Corbet Av. Shopping Cen. NR6 —5G **15**
Corie Rd. NR4 —4G **23**
Corncutters Clo. NR3 —3C **2**
Corner La. NR10 —2G **7**
Cornwallis Clo. NR5 —2B **22**
Coronation Clo. NR6 —3H **13**
Coronation Rd. NR6 —4H **13**

Coslany Sq. NR3 —3B 2
Coslany St. NR3 —3C 24 (3B 2)
Cossgrove Clo. NR3 —4A 14
Costessey La. NR8 —1H 11
Costessey Rd. NR8 —5F 5
Cotman Fields. NR1
(in two parts) —2E 25 (2F 2)
Cotman Rd. NR1 —4G 25
Cottage Dri., The. NR7 —1B 26
Cotterall Ct. NR5 —2C 22
Cottinghams Dri. NR6 —1F 13
Coughtrey Clo. NR7 —3G 15
Courtenay Clo. NR5 —1A 22
Covey, The. NR8 —3G 5
Cowdewell M. NR8 —3G 5
Cowgate. NR3 —2D 24 (1C 2)
Cow Hill. NR2 —3C 24 (4A 2)
Cozens Hardy Rd. NR7 —3G 15
Cozens Rd. NR1 —5F 25
Cranage Rd. NR1 —2D 34
Cranleigh Rise. NR4 —2G 33
Cranwell Gdns. NR14 —4E 39
Cranworth Gdns. NR1 —5C 24
Craske M. NR5 —1G 21
Creance Rd. NR7 —3H 15
Cremorne La. NR1 —4G 25
Crescent, The. NR2
—4C 24 (6A 3)
Crescent, The. NR8 —5A 6
Crescent, The. NR9 —6C 30
Cressener Clo. NR6 —2F 13
Cresswell Clo. NR5 —3C 22
Cricket Clo. NR10 —2H 5
Cricketfield View. NR13 —5G 29
Cricket Ground Rd. NR1 —6D 24
Cringleford Chase. NR4 —2D 32
Critoph Clo. NR14 —5D 38
Croftholme Way. NR1 —6H 15
Crofts, The. NR5 —2A 22
Croft, The. NR8 —2A 12
Crome Rd. NR3 —6E 15
Cromer Rd. NR6 —1H 13
Cromes Oak Clo. NR14 —5C 38
Cromwell Clo. NR9 —4D 30
Cromwell Rd. NR7 —4G 15
Crooks Pl. NR1 —5C 24 (7A 3)
Cross La. NR3 —2C 2
Cross St. NR3 —2C 24 (1B 2)
Crostwick La. NR10 —2F 9
Crowes Loke. NR13 —2C 18
Crown Rd. NR1 —3D 24 (4D 2)
Crown Rd. NR5 —6C 12
Crown Rd. NR10 —2A 8
Crummock Rd. NR5 —3D 22
Cubitt Rd. NR1 —2H 25
Cuckoo La. NR13 —5H 29
Cucumber La. NR13 —2D 28
Culling's Hill. NR13 —5H 27
Culverin Clo. NR7 —1E 27
Cunningham Rd. NR5 —4D 22
Curson Clo. NR9 —5C 30
Cursons M. NR18 —2C 36
Curtis Rd. NR6 —3A 14
Custance Ct. NR4 —6F 23
Cuthbert Clo. NR7 —3G 15
Cutler Way. NR5 —1G 21
Cuttons Corner. NR13 —4H 19
Cypress Clo. NR8 —5H 5
Cyprus St. NR1 —6D 24
Cyril Rd. NR7 —2C 26

Dacre Clo. NR4 —2F 33
Dakin Rd. NR3 —5C 14
Dales Loke. NR7 —4A 26
Dales Pl. NR7 —4C 26
Dales, The. NR13 —4F 29
Dalrymple Way. NR6 —3B 14
Damgate Ct. NR18 —5C 36
Damgate St. NR18 —5C 36
Damocles Ct. NR2
—3C 24 (4A 2)
Danby Clo. NR4 —3A 34
Danesbower Clo. NR13 —2H 29
Danesbower La. NR13 —1H 29
Daniels Rd. NR4 —6A 24
Darrell Pl. NR5 —2E 23
Dately Ct. NR2 —3H 23
Davey Pl. NR2 —5B 3
Davidson Clo. NR7 —2C 26
Davidson Rd. NR7 —2C 26
Dawson Ct. NR1 —6C 24
Deacon Clo. NR13 —3F 29
Deacon Dri. NR9 —4E 31
De Caux Rd. NR3 —6D 14
Deepdale. NR13 —4F 29
Deep Rd. NR18 —1C 36
De Hague Rd. NR4 —5G 23
Delane Rd. NR8 —6D 6
Dell Cres. NR5 —2F 23
Dell Loke. NR14 —1G 35
Dell, The. NR14 —1G 35
Deloney Rd. NR7 —5H 15
Delta Clo. NR6 —3B 14
Denbigh Ho. NR2 —3A 24
Denbigh Rd. NR2 —4A 24
Denes, The. NR7 —4H 25
Denmark Opening. NR3 —6D 14
Denmark Rd. NR3 —6D 14
Denmead Clo. NR4 —3H 33
Dennis Rd. NR6 —6G 7
Denton Rd. NR3 —4E 15
Derby St. NR2 —2B 24
Dereham Rd. NR2 —2G 23
Dereham Rd. NR5 —5E 11
Dereham Rd. NR9 —5A 10
Dersley Ct. NR5 —2H 21
Desmond Dri. NR6 —1E 15
Devon Av. NR6 —3F 13
Devonshire St. NR2 —2A 24
Dewing Rd. NR13 —1F 17
Dial Ho. NR1 —8A 3
Diamond Rd. NR6 —2A 14
Dian Rd. NR13 —4G 29
Dibden Rd. NR3 —1E 25
Distillery Sq. NR2 —3B 24
Dixon Rd. NR7 —3F 15
Dixons Fold. NR6 —3E 15
Doctors Rd. NR13 —1G 29
Dodderman Way. NR5 —4B 22
Dog La. NR10 —1B 6
Dogwood Rd. NR6 —3C 14
Dolphin Gro. NR2 —1A 24
Dolphin Path. NR2 —1B 24
Doman Rd. NR1 —5E 25 (8E 3)
Donchurch Clo. NR5 —2B 22
Donkey La. NR4 —2G 33
Don Pratt Ct. NR3 —1E 2
Doris Rd. NR2 —4A 24
Doughty's Hospital. NR3 —2C 2
Douglas Clo. NR6 —6C 8
Douglas Haig Rd. NR5 —3E 23
Douglas Rd. NR10 —3F 9
Douro Pl. NR2 —3B 24
Dovedales. NR6 —3E 15
Dovedales Ct. NR6 —3E 15
Dover St. NR2 —4A 24
Dove St. NR2 —4B 2
Dowding Rd. NR6 —1C 14
(in two parts)
Downham Cres. NR18 —2D 36
Downing M. NR5 —1G 21
Dowson Rd. NR3 —6A 14
Dragoon St. NR3 —1E 25
Drake Clo. NR9 —4E 31
Draper Way.. NR5 —1G 21
Drayton Gro. NR8 —5A 6
Drayton High Rd. NR8 & NR6
—5B 6
Drayton Ind. Est. NR8 —5A 6
Drayton La. NR10 —3D 6
Drayton Lodge Pk. NR8 —6C 6
Drayton Rd. NR3 —5G 13
Drayton Wood Rd. NR6 —1E 13
Drewray Dri. NR8 —2H 5
Drive, The. NR5 —6C 12
Drive, The. NR14 —1H 35
Drury Clo. NR5 —1C 22
Dryden Rd. NR8 —5G 5
Duckett Clo. NR1 —2D 34
Duff Rd. NR3 —5C 14
Dugard Av. NR1 —1G 25
Duke St. NR3 —2C 24 (2B 2)
Dunston Cotts. NR1 —8F 3
Dunwood Dri. NR6 —6E 9
Durham St. NR2 —5A 24
Dussindale. NR18 —2D 36
Dussindale Dri. NR7 —5E 17
Duverlin Clo. NR4 —2H 33
Dye's Rd. NR13 —2D 18

Eade Rd. NR3 —1C 24
Eagle Wlk. NR2 —5B 24
Eagle Way. NR9 —4E 31
Earlham Ct. NR2 —3B 24
Earlham Grn. La. NR5 —2A 22
(in two parts)
Earlham Gro. NR5 —3E 23
Earlham Ho. NR2 —4H 23
Earlham Rd. NR2 —3G 23
Earlham Rd. NR4 —4D 22
Earlham W. Cen. NR5 —3D 22
East Av. NR13 —4G 29
Eastbourne Pl. NR1
—3E 25 (4E 2)
Eastern Av. NR7 —2D 26
Eastern Clo. NR7 —2D 26
Eastern Cres. NR7 —2D 26
Eastern Rd. NR7 —2D 26
Eastfield. NR8 —5G 5
Easton Rd. NR9 —1A 20
Eastwood M. NR6 —4D 14
Eaton Cen. NR4 —2F 33
Eaton Chase. NR4 —1F 33
Eaton Rd. NR4 —1A 34
Eaton St. NR4 —3F 33
Ebbisham Dri. NR4 —2G 33
Ebenezer Pl. NR3 —1C 24 (1A 2)
Ecton Wlk. NR6 —2E 15
Eden Clo. NR7 —3H 25
Edgefield Clo. NR6 —6E 9
Edgeworth Rd. NR5 —3D 22
Edinburgh Rd. NR2 —3H 23
Edmund Bacon Ct. NR3 —1C 24
Edrich Clo. NR13 —1G 29
Edward Gambling Ct. NR2
—1A 24
Edwards Rd. NR7 —2F 15
Edward St. NR3 —1C 24 (1C 2)
Edwin Clo. NR18 —3C 36
Eleanor Rd. NR1 —6C 24
Elizabeth Av. NR7 —2C 26
Elizabeth Clo. NR7 —2G 15
Elizabeth Clo. NR10 —1F 9
Elizabeth Fry Rd. NR2 —4G 23
Elizabeth Rd. NR14 —5C 38
Elkins Rd. NR18 —3C 36
Ella Rd. NR1 —3F 25
Ellcar Rise. NR4 —2H 33
Ellis Gdns. NR4 —6G 33
Elm Clo. NR5 —5A 12
Elmdon Ct. NR1 —3F 25
Elm Gro. La. NR3 —5C 14
Elm Hill. NR3 —3D 24 (3C 2)
Elms, The. NR2 —4A 24
Elms, The. NR6 —1D 14
Elstead Clo. NR4 —3G 33
Elveden Clo. NR4 —2G 33
Elvina Rd. NR10 —2F 9
Elvin Way. NR3 —6G 13
Elwyn Rd. NR1 —1D 34
Ely St. NR2 —2B 24
Embry Cres. NR6 —1C 14
Enfield Rd. NR5 —3D 22
English Rd. NR6 —3D 14
Ernest Clo. NR8 —3H 5
Esdelle St. NR3 —1C 24
Esperanto Way. NR2 —5B 3
Essex St. NR2 —4B 24
Estelle Way. NR18 —2F 37
Ethel Gooch Rd. NR18 —3C 36
Ethel Rd. NR1 —4F 25
Europa Way. NR1 —1F 35
Eustace Rd. NR3 —4H 13
Eva Rd. NR13 —1G 17
Eversley Rd. NR6 —3A 14
Everson Clo. NR5 —6D 12
Exchange St. NR2 —3C 24 (4B 2)
Exeter St. NR2 —2B 24
Exmouth Clo. NR9 —4E 31

Fairfax Dri. NR7 —1E 27
Fairfax Rd. NR4 —5G 23
Fairfield Rd. NR2 —6B 24
Fairhaven Ct. NR2 —3H 23
Fairland St. NR18 —5D 36
Fairmile Clo. NR2 —6A 24
Fairstead Ct. NR7 —4F 15
Fairstead Rd. NR7 —4F 15
Fairview Clo. NR8 —6B 6
Fairways. NR6 —2E 13
Fakenham Rd. NR8 —1A 4
Falcon M. NR7 —3H 15
Falcon Rd. E. NR7 —4H 15
Falcon Rd. W. NR7 —3G 15
Falkland Clo. NR6 —2E 13
Fallowfield Clo. NR1 —1G 25
Fallows, The. NR8 —3G 5
Farmers Av. NR1 —4D 24 (5C 3)
Farmland Rd. NR5 —5A 12
Farrow Rd. NR5 —3G 23
Fastolf Clo. NR6 —2F 13
Fellowes Clo. NR5 —3E 23
Felsham Way. NR8 —2H 5
Fenn Cres. NR3 —6A 14
Fern Ct. NR18 —4C 36
Ferndale Clo. NR6 —3F 13
Fernhill. NR1 —4G 25
Ferry La. NR13 —5H 27
Ferry Rd. NR1 —3E 25 (4F 2)
Ferry Rd. NR14 —5B 28
Fiddlewood Rd. NR6 —3C 14
Fieldfare Clo. NR10 —3G 9
Fielding Ct. NR16 —6C 24
Field La. NR13 —5G 19
Field Rd. NR8 —5A 4
Fieldview. NR5 —3F 23
Fifers La. NR6 —1H 13
Finch Clo. NR7 —5A 16
Finchley Ct. NR2 —2A 24
Finch Way. NR13 —4E 29
Finderne Dri. NR18 —2E 37
Finkelgate. NR1 —5D 24 (8D 3)
Fiona Clo. NR18 —2F 37
Fir Covert Rd. NR8 —3E 5
Firethorn Clo. NR8 —3E 5
Firman Ct. NR7 —1C 26
Firs Rd. NR6 —1G 13
Firs Rd. NR9 —5C 30
Fir Tree Clo. NR13 —3D 28
Firtree Rd. NR7 —6B 16
Firwood Clo. NR1 —1H 25
Fishergate. NR3 —2D 24 (2C 2)
Fisher's Clo. NR5 —6H 11
Fishers La. NR2 —3C 24 (4A 2)
Fitzgerald Rd. NR1 —2D 34
Fitzgerald Rd. NR14 —3D 38
Fitzhenry M. NR5 —1C 22
Fitzmaurice Ct. NR13 —6B 14
Fleet Rd. NR8 —1D 10
Fletcher Way. NR3 —4B 14
Florence Rd. NR1 —3F 25
Flowerdew Clo. NR9 —5C 30
Folgate Clo. NR8 —2A 12
Folgate La. NR8 —2A 12
Folly Clo. NR18 —3D 36
Folly Gdns. NR18 —3D 36
Folly Rd. NR18 —3D 36
Folwell Rd. NR5 —6H 11
Footpath, The. NR14 —4C 38
Forester Clo. NR4 —2B 34
Forge Clo. NR14 —5D 38
Fortune Grn. NR14 —5H 39
Foster Clo. NR13 —3D 28
Foster Rd. NR3 —4C 14
Foulgers Ho. NR1 —7E 3
Foulgers Opening. NR1
—5E 25 (8E 3)
Fountain Ct. NR1 —8A 3
Fountains Rd. NR4 —3B 34
Fowell Clo. NR5 —3C 22
Foxburrow Rd. NR7 —2F 15
Foxcotte Clo. NR6 —6F 7
Fox La. NR13 —1H 29
Fox La. NR14 —1D 38
Foxley Clo. NR5 —3E 23
Fox Rd. NR14 —1D 38
Foxwood Clo. NR8 —2H 5
Framingham Earl La. NR14
—3G 39
Framingham Rd. NR14 —1G 39
Frances Ct. NR2 —3A 24
Francis La. NR13 —3F 19
Francis Way. NR5 —6H 11
Freeland Clo. NR8 —2H 5
Freeman Sq. NR2 —1B 24
Frenbury Est. NR6 —4G 13
Frensham Rd. NR3 —6G 13
Frere Rd. NR7 —6A 16
Fresher M. NR5 —3A 22
Freshfield Clo. NR5 —2D 22
Freshwater Way. NR8 —2A 6
Friarscroft La. NR18 —5C 36
Friars Quay. NR3 —3D 24 (3C 2)
Friar Tuck Rd. NR4 —2B 34
Friends Rd. NR5 —3D 22
Frogs Hall La. NR1 —4G 25
Frogshall La. NR18 —3B 36
Frogs Hole. NR13 —1F 29
Frost Clo. NR7 —1C 26
Frost Ind. Pk. NR8 —6C 6
Fugill Grn. NR7 —6A 16
Fugill Rd. NR7 —5A 16
Fuller M. NR5 —1H 21
Fulton Clo. NR4 —2H 33
Furze Av. NR7 —1B 26
Furze Rd. NR7 —6B 16
Fye Bri. NR3 —2C 2
Fye Bri St. NR3 —2D 24 (2C 2)

Gaffers Ct. NR2 —4A 2
Gage Rd. NR7 —3H 15
Galley Hill. NR3 —5H 13
Gamewell Clo. NR1 —1D 34
Ganners Hill. NR8 —2H 5
Gaol Hill. NR2 —3C 24 (4B 2)
Gardeners Ter. NR7 —4E 15
Garden Pl. NR3 —1D 24
Garden Rd. NR13 —1G 29
Garden St. NR1 —4D 24 (6D 3)
Gardyn Croft. NR8 —3G 5
Gargle Hill. NR7 —2C 26
Garrett Ct. NR3 —6E 15
Garrick Grn. NR6 —2D 14
Gas Hill. NR1 —3F 25
Gateley Gdns. NR3 —4B 14
Gawdy Rd. NR7 —6H 15
Gaynor Clo. NR18 —2B 36
Gayton Wlk. NR6 —1E 15
Gentlemans Wlk. NR2
—4C 24 (4B 2)
Gentry Pl. NR5 —1D 22
Geoffrey Rd. NR1 —6E 25
George Borrow Rd. NR4 —4F 23
George Carver Ct. NR4 —5F 23
George Clo. NR8 —5C 6
George Dri. NR8 —6C 6
George Fox Way. NR5 —4D 22
George Hill. NR6 —3D 14
George Pope Clo. NR3 —5B 14
George Pope Rd. NR3 —5B 14
George Winter Ct. NR3 —5B 14
Gerald Clo. NR1 —1H 25
Gerard Hudson Gdns. NR4
—6G 33
Gertrude Rd. NR3 —6E 15
Gibbs Clo. NR9 —1E 31
Gilbard Rd. NR5 —2D 22
Gilbert Clo. NR14 —5H 39
Gilbert Way. NR4 —2E 33
Gilchrist Clo. NR4 —3C 34
Gildencroft. NR3 —2C 24 (1B 2)
Giles Rd. NR10 —3G 9
Gilman Rd. NR3 —6E 15
Gipsy Clo. NR5 —3E 23
Gipsy La. NR5 —4E 23
Girlings La. NR7 —4B 26
Girton Rd. NR2 —5A 24
Glade, The. NR8 —3A 12
Gladstone St. NR2 —3A 24
Glebe Clo. NR8 —4A 6
Glebe Rd. NR2 —5H 23
Glenalmond. NR4 —1H 33
Glenburn Av. NR7 —3F 15
Glenburn Ct. NR7 —3F 15
Glenda Clo. NR5 —6D 12
Glenda Ct. NR5 —5D 12
Glenda Cres. NR5 —5D 12
Glenda Rd. NR5 —6D 12
Glendenning Rd. NR1 —4G 25
Glengarry Clo. NR9 —4C 30
Glenmore Gdns. NR3 —5A 14
Glenn Rd. NR14 —6C 38
Globe La. NR13 —1G 29
Globe Pl. NR2 —4B 24
Gloucester St. NR2 —5A 24
Godfrey Rd. NR10 —2G 9
Godric Pl. NR2 —3G 23
Golden Ball St. NR1
—4D 24 (6C 3)
Golden Dog La. NR3
—2D 24 (2C 2)
Golding Pl. NR2 —3B 24
Goldsmith St. NR2 —2B 24
Goldwell Rd. NR1 —5D 24
Goodhale Rd. NR5 —2C 22
Goodman Sq. NR2 —2A 24
Goodwood Clo. NR7 —6B 16
Gordon Av. NR7 —2H 25
Gordon Godfrey Way. NR10
—2F 7
Gordon Rd. NR1 —5D 24 (8D 3)
Gordon Sq. NR1 —5D 24 (8D 3)
Gorse Av. NR6 —2H 13
Gorse Rd. NR7 —1A 26
Goulburn Rd. NR7 —6A 16
Gould Rd. NR2 —5G 23
Gowing Clo. NR6 —6G 7
Gowing Ct. NR3 —4A 14
Gowing Rd. NR6 —6G 7
Grace Jarrold Ct. NR3 —2C 2
Graham Sq. NR7 —6A 16
Grange Clo. NR6 —3D 14
Grange Clo. NR12 —1D 40
Grange Rd. NR2 —5H 23
Grange Wlk. NR12 —3B 40
Grant Rd. NR10 —2G 9

Grant St. NR2 —2H 23
Grapes Hill. NR2 —3B 24
Grasmere. NR9 —4E 31
Grasmere Clo. NR5 —3D 22
Gravelfield Clo. NR1 —1G 25
Gt. Melton Rd. NR9 —4C 30
(Hethersett)
Gt. Melton Rd. NR9 —1D 30
(Little Melton)
Greenacre Clo. NR13 —3E 29
Greenacres Dri. NR14 —3B 38
Greenborough Clo. NR7 —5B 16
Greenborough Rd. NR7 —5B 16
Green Clo. NR5 —6H 11
Green Ct. NR7 —2A 26
Green Fall. NR14 —5D 38
Greenfields. NR5 —6G 11
Greenhills Clo. NR8 —3A 12
Greenhills Rd. NR3 —1C 24
Greenland Av. NR18 —2F 37
Green La. NR9 —5F 21
Green La. E. NR13 —2F 17
Green La. N. NR13 —5E 17
Green La. S. NR7 —3F 27
Green La. S. NR13 —6F 17
Green La. W. NR13 —1F 17
Green Pk. Rd. NR10 —2G 7
Green, The. NR8 —5B 6
Greenways. NR4 —2G 33
Greenwood Rd. NR4 —2C 34
Greenwood Way. NR7 —5C 16
Grenville Clo. NR9 —4F 31
Gresham Rd. NR3 —5H 13
Greyfriars Clo. NR6 —2D 14
Greyfriars Rd. NR1 —3D 24 (4D 2)
Greyhound Opening. NR2 —2B 24
Griffin La. NR7 —3E 27
Gristock Pl. NR5 —1D 22
Grosvenor Rd. NR2 —4B 24
Grouts Throughfare. NR1 —5C 3
Grove Av. NR1 —5C 24 (8A 3)
Grove Av. NR5 —6A 12
Grovebury Clo. NR13 —3E 29
Grovedale Clo. NR5 —6B 12
Grove Rd. NR1 —5C 24 (8A 3)
Grove Rd. NR9 —4D 30
Grove, The. NR3 —4C 14
Grove Wlk. NR1 —6C 24
Guardian Rd. NR5 —2G 23
Guardian Rd. Ind. Est. NR5 —3F 23
Guelph Rd. NR1 —3F 25
Guernsey Rd. NR3 —1D 24
Guildhall Hill. NR2 —3C 24 (4B 2)
Gull La. NR14 —3E 39
Gunn Rd. NR7 —6H 15
Gunns Ct. NR2 —3B 24
Gunton La. NR5 —5C 12
Gunton Rd. NR2 —4G 23
Gunton Rd. NR18 —4E 37
Gurney Clo. NR5 —1C 22
Gurney Ct. NR3 —2C 2
Gurney Ct. NR5 —1B 22
Gurney Dri. NR7 —4A 16
Gurney La. NR4 —1D 32
Gurney Rd. NR1 —2F 25
Gurney Rd. NR5 —6B 12

Haconsfield. NR9 —4E 31
Hadden Clo. NR14 —4D 38
Haig Clo. NR5 —3E 23
Halcombe Ct. NR3 —6D 14
Halden Av. NR6 —1G 13
Hales Ct. NR2 —4C 24 (5A 3)
Half Mile Clo. NR3 —5A 14
Half Mile Rd. NR3 —5A 14
Half Moon Way. NR2 —1A 24
Hallback La. NR14 —6G 35
Hall Clo. NR9 —5E 31
Hall Dri. NR5 —5G 11
Hall Farm Pl. NR9 —3E 21
Hallgate. NR13 —4E 17
Hall La. NR8 —5B 6
Hall Rd. NR4 & NR1 —4B 34 (8D 3)
Hall Rd. NR5 —5B 12
Hall Rd. NR9 —6A 10
(Easton)
Hall Rd. NR9 —2A 30
(Hethersett)
Hall Rd. NR13 —5D 18
(Little Plumstead)
Hall Rd. NR13 —1C 28
(Witton)
Hall Rd. NR14 —4E 39
Hamlin Ct. NR3 —5A 14
Hammond Clo. NR7 —4B 16
Hammond Way. NR7 —4B 16
Hamond Rd. NR6 —2E 13
Hampden Dri. NR7 —1E 27
Hanbury Clo. NR5 —4E 23
Hancock Ct. NR5 —2H 21
Hankin Ct. NR5 —4D 22
Hanly Clo. NR7 —6H 15
Hanover Rd. NR2 —5B 24
Hansard Clo. NR3 —6A 14
Hansard La. NR3 —2D 24 (2D 2)
Hansard Rd. NR3 —5A 14
Hansell Rd. NR7 —1C 26
Harbord Rd. NR4 —4G 23
Harbour Rd. NR1 —4F 25
Harcourt Clo. NR3 —1E 25
Hardesty Clo. NR14 —4C 38
Hardwick Clo. NR4 —3H 33
Hardy Rd. NR1 —5F 25
Hare Rd. NR13 —4H 17
Harewood Dri. NR8 —2H 5
Harford Hill. NR4 —4B 34
Harford Mnr. Clo. NR2 —1B 34
Harford St. NR1 —6D 24
Harker Way. NR13 —3G 19
Harlington Av. NR6 —3H 13
Harman Clo. NR9 —4E 31
Harmer Clo. NR4 —2E 33
Harmer Cres. NR4 —2D 32
Harmer La. NR4 —2D 32
Harmer Rd. NR3 —4B 14
Harpsfield. NR5 —1H 21
Harrier Way. NR6 —6C 8
Harrisons Dri. NR7 —4B 16
Harrold Clo. NR8 —3H 5
Harry Barber Clo. NR5 —1B 22
Harry Percival Clo. NR4 —1B 34
Harsnet Clo. NR5 —1A 22
Harts La. NR4 —2D 32
Harts La. NR9 —2D 20
Hartwell Rd. NR12 —3B 40
Harvey Clo. NR7 —2H 25
Harvey Clo. NR9 —5C 30
Harvey La. NR7 —3H 25
Harwood Rd. NR1 —2D 34
Haslips Clo. NR2 —2B 24
Hassett Clo. NR3 —1E 25
Hastings Av. NR6 —3H 13
Hatton Rd. NR1 —6D 24
Hauteyn Ct. NR3 —5B 14
Havant Clo. NR4 —2F 33
Havelock Rd. NR2 —3A 24
Haverscroft Clo. NR8 —3G 5
Havers Rd. NR3 —6A 14
Hawthorn Clo. NR10 —3F 9
Hawthorne Av. NR6 —2H 13
Hawthorne Clo. NR18 —2E 37
Hawthorne Row. NR2 —2A 24
Hawthorn La. NR2 —6A 24
Hawthorn Rd. NR5 —5B 12
Hayden Ct. NR1 —6D 24
Hay Hill. NR2 —5B 3
Haymarket. NR2 —4C 24 (5B 3)
Hazel Clo. NR8 —4H 5
Hazel Rd. NR5 —5A 12
Heartsease La. NR7 —6G 15
Heath Clo. NR6 —1A 14
Heath Clo. NR10 —2F 7
Heath Cres. NR6 —2H 13
Heather Av. NR6 —3H 13
Heatherwood Clo. NR13 —4E 17
Heathgate. NR3 —2F 25
Heath Loke. NR14 —4B 38
Heath Rd. NR3 —1C 24
Heath Rd. NR13 —5E 17
Heathside Rd. NR1 —4G 25
Heath Way. NR13 —4E 19
(in two parts)
Hedgerows, The. NR5 —2B 22
Heigham Gro. NR2 —3B 24
Heigham Rd. NR2 —3A 24
Heigham St. NR2 —1A 24
Heigham Watering. NR2 —1A 24
Helena Rd. NR2 —3A 24
Helford St. NR2 —1A 24
Helgate Ct. NR2 —3A 2
Hellesdon Clo. NR6 —1E 23
Hellesdon Hall Rd. NR6 —6F 13
Hellesdon M. NR6 —5E 13
Hellesdon Mill La. NR6 —6E 13
Hellesdon Pk. Ind. Est. NR1 —5F 13
Hellesdon Pk. Rd. NR6 —4F 13
Hellesdon Rd. NR6 —1E 23
Hemblington Hall Rd. NR13 —3H 19
Hemlin Clo. NR5 —3D 22
Hemmings Clo. NR5 —2A 22
Hempsted M. NR5 —2H 21
Henby Way. NR7 —2A 26
Henderson Rd. NR4 —4G 23
Hendon Clo. NR5 —6C 12
Henley Rd. NR2 —5H 23
Henstead Rd. NR9 —4D 30
Herbert Nursey Clo. NR8 —6D 6
Hercules Clo. NR6 —3G 13
Hercules Rd. NR6 —3G 13
Herrick Rd. NR8 —5G 5
Hethersett Ho. NR9 —4D 30
Hethersett La. NR4 —2H 31
Hethersett Rd. NR9 —3A 30
Hewett Yd. NR1 —1C 34
Hewitts La. NR18 —3D 36
Higham Clo. NR7 —4F 15
Highfield. NR13 —2C 18
Highfield Av. NR13 —4F 29
Highfield Clo. NR7 —3D 26
Highfield Rd. NR8 —4A 6
Highfields. NR5 —6G 11
High Grn. NR1 —4G 25
High Grn. NR9 —4A 30
Highgrove Ct. NR14 —2B 38
High Ho. Av. NR18 —3E 37
High Ho. Clo. NR18 —3E 37
Highland. NR14 —1A 38
Highland Av. NR2 —5H 23
Highland Rd. NR2 —5H 23
Highland Rd. NR8 —5G 5
Highlands. NR8 —3A 12
Highlow Rd. NR5 —6B 12
Highview Clo. NR13 —1G 29
Hilary Av. NR1 —1G 25
Hill Crest. NR5 —5B 12
Hill Crest Rd. NR7 —2A 26
Hill Farm Clo. NR4 —3E 33
Hill Ho. Rd. NR1 —4F 25
Hillmead. NR3 —4C 14
Hill Rd. NR5 —5B 12
Hill Rd. NR7 —6C 16
Hillside. NR14 —3B 38
Hillside Av. NR7 —3C 26
Hillside Clo. NR7 —3C 26
Hillside Rd. NR7 —3C 26
Hills Rd. NR5 —6H 11
Hill St. NR2 —5B 24
Hill Top Dri. NR8 —4A 12
Hillvue Clo. NR5 —5B 12
Hilly Plantation. NR7 —2B 26
Hinshalwood Way. NR8 —3H 11
Hobart Clo. NR18 —2E 37
Hobart La. NR1 —6D 24 (8D 3)
Hobart Sq. NR1 —5D 24 (8D 3)
Hobrough La. NR1 —4E 25 (6E 3)
Hockering La. NR9 —3E 21
Hodgson Rd. NR4 —4G 23
Hog Bog La. NR10 —1D 8
Holland Ct. NR1 —3E 25 (4E 2)
Holls La. NR1 —5D 24 (8D 3)
Holly Bank. NR7 —5F 15
Holly Dri. NR2 —2H 23
Holly La. NR13 —5F 19
Holmes Clo. NR7 —1A 26
Holmesdale Rd. NR13 —3D 28
Holmwood Rise. NR7 —3H 25
Holt Rd. NR10 & NR6 —1F 7
Holworthy Rd. NR5 —1C 22
Honey Clo. NR1 —2G 25
Honeycombe Rd. NR13 —1C 18
Honingham La. NR8 —5A 4
Hooker Rd. NR7 —6A 16
Hooper La. NR3 —5E 15
Hopton Clo. NR7 —1E 27
Hornbeam Clo. NR7 —3A 16
Horning Clo. NR5 —2E 23
Horning Rd. NR12 —2C 40
Hornor Clo. NR2 —6B 24
Horns La. NR1 —4D 24 (7D 3)
Horsbeck Way. NR10 —2F 7
Horsefair, The. NR1 —4E 2
Horseshoe Clo. NR5 —6H 11
Horsford St. NR2 —1A 24
Hospital La. NR1 —6D 24
Hospital La. NR6 —4E 13
Hospital Rd. NR13 —5B 18
Hotblack Rd. NR2 —2H 23
Houghton Clo. NR5 —1C 22
Howard Clo. NR7 —2A 26
Howard M. NR3 —6D 14
Howard Ter. NR1 —1C 24
Howe La. NR14 —6D 38
Howell Rd. NR8 —6D 6
Howes Clo. NR9 —5D 30
Howlett Dri. NR5 —1B 22
Hubbard Clo. NR18 —2B 36
Hubbards Loke. NR9 —5C 30
Hudson Way. NR5 —2H 21
Hughenden Rd. NR1 —6D 24
Hughes Ct. NR9 —4E 31
Humbleyard. NR5 —1B 22
Hunt Clo. NR6 —6D 8
Hunter Rd. NR3 —4B 14
Hunters Clo. NR13 —2H 29
Huntingfield. NR5 —6A 12
Huntingfield Clo. NR5 —6A 12
Hurd Rd. NR4 —6G 23
Hurn Rd. NR8 —6D 6
Hurricane Way. NR6 —1A 14
Hutchinson Rd. NR5 —3E 23
Huxley Clo. NR1 —1E 35
Huxley Rd. NR1 —1E 35

Ice Ho. La. NR1 —5E 25 (8F 3)
Ilex Ct. NR7 —3A 16
Impala Clo. NR6 —1F 15
Ingram Ct. NR1 —6D 24
Inman Rd. NR7 —3A 16
Intwood Rd. NR4 —4E 33
Ipswich Gro. NR2 —5C 24 (8A 3)
Ipswich Rd. NR4, NR2 & NR1 —4B 34 (8A 3)
Ipswich Rd. NR14 —6A 34
Ireton Clo. NR7 —2E 27
Irstead Rd. NR5 —3F 23
Irving Rd. NR4 —2B 34
Isbets Dale. NR8 —3G 5
Ives Rd. NR6 —2C 14
Ivory Rd. NR4 —5F 23
Ivy Clo. NR14 —4D 38
Ivy Rd. NR10 —2F 9

James Alexander M. NR5 —4E 23
James Green Clo. NR10 —2G 9
Jamieson Pl. NR5 —1D 22
Jarrold Way. NR5 —1A 22
Jasmine Clo. NR4 —4F 23
Javelin Rd. NR6 —6B 8
Jay Gdns. NR5 —1H 21
Jenny Rd. NR10 —2G 9
Jerningham Rd. NR5 —6B 12
Jessopp Clo. NR2 —5G 23
Jessopp Rd. NR2 —5G 23
Jewson Rd. NR3 —5B 14
Jex Av. NR5 —1E 23
Jex La. NR5 —1E 23
Jex Rd. NR5 —1E 23
Joe Ellis Ct. NR5 —1C 22
John Drewry Clo. NR14 —3D 38
John Gale Ct. NR8 —2H 5
John Howes Clo. NR9 —5A 10
Johnson Pl. NR2 —4B 24
John Stephenson Ct. NR3
(off Gertude Rd.) —6E 15
Jolly Butcher's Yd. NR1 —7D 3
Jordan Clo. NR5 —3C 22
Jordan Clo. NR8 —1H 5
Josephine Clo. NR1 —6C 24
Jubilee Rd. NR7 —3F 15
Jubilee Ter. NR1 —6D 24
Judges Dri. NR4 —6G 23
Judges Gdns. NR8 —3H 5
Judges Wlk. NR4 —1G 33
Julian Rd. NR10 —2F 9
Junction Rd. NR3 —6B 14
Juniper Way. NR8 —3E 5
Jupiter Rd. NR6 —3B 14

Kabin Rd. NR5 —5C 12
Karen Clo. NR9 —6C 30
Keable Clo. NR5 —3E 23
Keats Rd. NR8 —5G 5
Kedelston Dri. NR4 —4D 32
Keelan Clo. NR6 —3A 14
Kempe Clo. NR7 —5H 15
Kendal Clo. NR9 —4E 31
Kennedy Clo. NR9 —5A 10
Kennett Clo. NR4 —5G 23
Kensington Pl. NR1 —5D 24 (8D 3)
Kered Clo. NR6 —1G 13
Kered Rd. NR6 —1G 13
Kerridges, The. NR5 —6A 12
Kerrison Rd. NR1 —5F 25
Kerville St. NR5 —2B 22
Kestrel Rd. NR7 —3H 15
Keswick Clo. NR4 —4E 33
Keswick Hall. NR4 —6G 33
Keswick Hall Rd. NR4 —6E 33
(in two parts)
Keswick Rd. NR4 —3E 33
Keswick Rd. NR7 —3F 15
Ketteringham La. NR9 —6D 30
Ketteringham Rd. NR18 —5G 37
Kett's Av. NR18 —3D 36
Kett's Clo. NR9 —5D 30
Kett's Clo. NR18 —3D 36
Kett's Hill. NR1 —2F 25
Kett's Oak. NR9 —6C 30
Keyes Clo. NR1 —1D 34
Keyes Rd. NR1 —1D 34
Keys Dri. NR12 —5A 40
Kiln Clo. NR6 —6D 8
Kiln Rd. NR10 —1F 7
Kimberley St. NR2 —4B 24
Kimberley St. NR18 —4D 36
Kinghorn Rd. NR2 —5G 23
Kingsgate Ct. NR2 —3C 24 (4A 2)
Kings Head La. NR3 —2B 2
Kings La. NR1 —5D 24 (7C 3)
Kingsley Rd. NR1 —5C 24 (7A 3)
Kingston Sq. NR4 —6H 23
King St. NR1 —3D 24 (4D 2)
Kingsway. NR2 —1B 24
Kingswood Av. NR8 —3G 5
Kingswood Clo. NR4 —3G 33
Kingswood Ct. NR8 —3G 5
Kinsale Av. NR6 —2F 13
Kinver Clo. NR4 —6A 24
Kirby Rd. NR14 —1H 35
(in two parts)
Kirklands. NR8 —3H 11
Kirklees. NR4 —4B 34
Kirkpatrick Rd. NR3 —5A 14
Knights Rd. NR3 —5A 14
Knowland Gro. NR5 —1D 22
Knowsley Rd. NR3 —1D 24
Knox Av. NR1 —1G 25
Knox Clo. NR1 —1G 25
Knox Rd. NR1 —2G 25

Laburnum Av. NR8 —4E 5
Laburnum Clo. NR10 —1F 7
Laburnum Dri. NR13 —1G 29
Lacey Rd. NR8 —4G 5
Lackford Clo. NR13 —3E 29
Ladbroke Pl. NR1 —2F 25
Lady Betty Rd. NR1 —6C 24
Lady Mary Rd. NR1 —6C 24
Lady's La. NR18 —5B 36
Lady Smith Rd. NR3 —6E 15
Lakeland Way. NR9 —4F 31
Lakenfields. NR1 —1E 35
Lakenham Rd. NR4 —1B 34
Lake View Dri. NR13 —3D 28
Lambert Ho. NR5 —1B 22
(off Humble Yd.)
Lambert Rd. NR7 —4F 15
Lancaster Clo. NR6 —1C 14
Lanchester Ct. NR2 —2A 24
Landlow La. NR9 —6A 20
Lanes Yd. NR1 —5D 3
Lane, The. NR3 —5A 14
Langham Grn. NR13 —3G 29
Langham Pl. NR1 —5C 24
Langley Clo. NR4 —4D 32
Langley Wlk. NR2 —2A 24
Langton Clo. NR5 —2C 22
Lansdowne Rd. NR6 —1A 14
Larch Clo. NR7 —3A 16
Larkman La. NR5 —2D 22
Lathes, The. NR3 —1B 2
Latimer Rd. NR1 —1D 34
Laud Clo. NR7 —2E 27
Laundry Clo. NR7 —2B 26
Laundry La. NR7 —3A 16
(Sprowston)
Laundry La. NR7 —2C 26
(Thorpe St Andrew)
Laundry La. NR13 —4D 18
Laurel Ct. NR7 —6B 16
Laurel Dri. NR13 —4C 28
Laurel Rd. NR7 —6C 16

Lavender Clo. NR10 —1F 7
Lavengro Rd. NR3 —1E 25
Lawn Clo. NR10 —1D 6
Lawn Cres. NR13 —4F 17
Lawson Rd. NR3 —6D 14
Layer Clo. NR5 —2A 22
Layson Dri. NR3 —6D 14
Layton Clo. NR8 —6C 6
Leach's Turn. NR14 —6D 28
Leafyoak La. NR14 —6C 38
Leas Ct. NR6 —1E 23
Leeder Hill. NR13 —5H 27
Leewood Cres. NR5 —6D 12
Lefroy Rd. NR3 —4H 13
Leicester St. NR2 —5B 24
Leng Cres. NR4 —1F 33
Lenthall Clo. NR7 —1E 27
Leonards St. NR3 —1C 24
Leopard Clo. NR3 —3B 2 (1D 2)
Leopold Rd. NR4 —6H 23
Leopold Rd. NR4 —6H 23
Le Strange Clo. NR2 —4G 23
Letunder Clo. NR7 —2B 26
Leveson Rd. NR7 —4G 15
Levine Clo. NR13 —4D 28
Leyham Ct. NR5 —1B 22
Liberator Rd. NR6 —1B 14
Libra Ct. NR7 —3H 15
Lilac Clo. NR10 —1F 7
Lilburne Av. NR3 —5C 14
Lilian Clo. NR6 —3A 14
Lilian Rd. NR10 —1F 9
Lilly Ter. NR1 —5D 24 (7D 3)
Lily Ter. NR1 —7D 3
Lime Tree Av. NR7 —2H 25
Lime Tree Av. NR8 —3A 12
Lime Tree Av. NR18 —2E 37
Limetree Clo. NR10 —1D 6
Limetree Clo. NR18 —3E 37
Limetree Ct. NR8 —4E 5
Lime Tree Rd. NR2 —6A 24
Linacre Av. NR7 —4H 15
Linacre Clo. NR7 —4H 15
Linalls Dri. NR8 —3F 11
Lincoln St. NR2 —4A 24
Linden Dri. NR9 —5C 30
Linden Rd. NR5 —6D 12
Lindford Dri. NR4 —3G 33
Lindley Clo. NR6 —1D 14
Lindley Rd. NR9 —5C 30
Lindley St. NR1 —6D 24
Lindsay Rd. NR7 —3H 15
Linford Dri. NR4 —2B 34
Lings Clo. NR10 —2G 7
Lingwood Rd. NR13 —1H 29
Links Av. NR6 —2G 13
Links Av. NR13 —4G 29
Links Clo. NR6 —2G 13
Lintock Rd. NR3 —4C 14
Linton Ct. NR7 —4G 15
Linton Cres. NR7 —3G 15
Lion & Castle Yd. NR1 —6C 3
Lion Wood Rd. NR1 —2G 25
Lishman Rd. NR7 —5B 16
Lisle Rd. NR5 —2A 22
Lit. Armes St. NR2 —1H 23
Lit. Bethel St. NR2 —5A 3
Lit. Bethel St. NR2
　　　　—4C 24 (5A 3)
Lit. Bull Clo. NR3
　　　　—2D 24 (1C 2)
Lit. John Rd. NR4 —2B 34
Little La. NR10 —2G 7
Lit. London St. NR2
　　　　—3D 24 (4C 2)
Lit. Melton La. NR4 —6G 21
Lit. Melton Rd. NR9 —3D 30
Lit. Water La. NR3
　　　　—3D 24 (3C 2)
Littlewood La. NR12 —1D 40
Livingstone St. NR2 —2H 23
Lizard, The. NR14 —5E 37
Lloyd Rd. NR1 —2G 25
Lloyd Rd. NR8 —4E 5
Loaning, The. NR1 —6E 25
Lobster La. NR2 —3C 24 (4B 2)
Locksley Rd. NR4 —3B 34
Lock, The. NR5 —2F 23
Loddon Rd. NR14 —1F 39
Loddon Rd. NR14 —1H 35
(in three parts)
Lodge Breck. NR8 —6B 6
Lodge La. NR6 —6D 8
Lodge Pl. NR7 —3B 26
Lodore Av. NR6 —1H 13
Loke, The. NR4 —3F 33

Loke, The. NR5 —4H 11
(New Costessey)
Loke, The. NR5 —2F 23
(Norwich)
Loke, The. NR13 —1H 29
Lollards Rd. NR1 —3E 25 (3F 2)
London Rd. NR18 —6B 36
London St. NR2 —3C 24 (4C 2)
Lone Barn Rd. NR7 —4G 15
Longbow Clo. NR4 —2B 34
Long Dale. NR8 —3A 6
Longdell Hills. NR5 —5H 11
Longe Rd. NR6 —1E 15
Longfields Rd. NR7 —6D 16
Long Gro. NR4 —4G 23
Long John Hill. NR1 —1D 34
Longlands Dri. NR18 —2B 36
Long La. NR3 —3B 2
Long La. NR9 —2D 20
Long La. NR13 —3D 36
Long La. NR14 —4A 38
Longmead. NR1 —1D 34
Longmeadow. NR13 —4E 29
Long Rd. NR14 —3C 38
Long Row. NR3 —6C 14
Long's Cres. NR13 —1E 17
Longview. NR9 —3D 30
Longwater La. NR8 & NR5
　　　　—4G 11
Lonsdale Rd. NR13 —1G 17
Lorraine Gdns. NR3 —4D 14
Losinga Cres. NR3 —4A 14
Lothian St. NR2 —3B 24
Louis Clo. NR6 —1C 14
Louise Rd. NR4 —4G 23
Lovelace Rd. NR4 —5F 23
Lovett Clo. NR6 —1E 15
Lwr. Clarence Rd. NR1
　　　　—4E 25 (5F 3)
Lower Clo. NR1 —3E 25 (3E 2)
Lwr. Goat La. NR2 —4B 2
Loweswater Gdns. NR5 —3E 23
(off Douglas Haig Rd.)
Lowes Yd. NR3 —2C 2
Low Rd. NR4 —5F 33
Low Rd. NR8 & NR6 —6B 6
Low Rd. NR13 —6F 17
Lowry Cole Rd. NR6 —2E 15
Lowther Rd. NR4 —2A 34
Lox Wood. NR6 —6F 7
Loyalty Ct. NR1 —6B 3
Lubbock Clo. NR2 —4G 23
Lucerne Clo. NR6 —2E 15
Luke Clo. NR5 —1C 22
Lusher Rise. NR6 —1E 23
Lushers Loke. NR7 —1E 23
Lushington Clo. NR5 —1C 22
Lyhart Rd. NR4 —2A 34
Lynch Grn. NR9 —4C 30
Lynch Rd. NR9 —4D 30
Lyngate Clo. NR9 —5B 30
Lytton Rd. NR8 —5G 5

Mack's La. NR8 —6G 5
Madells Ct. NR3 —3C 2
Maden Clo. NR18 —3C 36
Magdalen Rd. NR3 —1D 24
Magdalen Rd. NR3 —1D 24
Magdalen St. NR3
　　　　—1D 24 (1C 2)
Magnay Rd. NR8 —6D 6
Magnolia Clo. NR18 —3C 36
Magpie Rd. NR3 —1C 24
Maidavale. NR2 —4A 24
Maid Marian Rd. NR4 —2B 34
Maidstone Rd. NR1 —4D 2
Malbrook Rd. NR5 —3C 22
Mallard Clo. NR1 —5G 29
Mallory Rd. NR6 —1C 14
Malten Clo. NR14 —5D 38
Malthouse La. NR1 —6B 3
Malthouse Rd. NR2
　　　　—4C 24 (6B 3)
Malthouse Rd. NR9 —4C 30
Malvern Rd. NR1 —2F 25
Malzy Ct. NR3 —1B 2
Manby Rd. NR7 —6H 15
Manchester Pl. NR2 —4B 24
Mancroft Wlk. NR2 —2B 24
Mandela Clo. NR3
　　　　—2C 24 (2A 2)
Manor Chase. NR8 —5H 5
Manor Clo. NR10 —1A 8
Manor Farm Clo. NR8 —5B 6

Manor Ridge. NR13 —1H 29
Manor Rd. NR10 —1A 8
Mansel Dri. NR6 —4D 14
Mansfield La. NR1 —1D 34
Manthorpe Clo. NR1 —2D 34
Mantle Clo. NR7 —3A 16
Maple Dri. NR2 —2G 23
Maple Clo. NR8 —3E 5
Maple Rd. NR18 —2E 37
Margaret Clo. NR6 —2E 13
Margaret Cres. NR7 —2C 26
Margaret Paston Av. NR3
　　　　—5H 13
Margaret Reeve Clo. NR18
　　　　—3E 37
Margaret Rd. NR5 —5C 12
Margetson Av. NR7 —2H 25
Marigold Clo. NR10 —1F 7
Mariners La. NR1
　　　　—5D 24 (7D 3)
Marion Clo. NR18 —3D 36
Marion Rd. NR1 —3F 25
Marion Roberts Ct. NR9 —5C 30
Marionville Rd. NR3 —4D 14
Marjorie Hinde Ct. NR2 —5A 3
Market Av. NR1 —4D 24 (4C 2)
Marketfield La. NR10 —1C 8
Market La. NR9 —2A 30
Market Pl. NR2 —4C 24 (5B 3)
Market St. NR18 —4C 36
Markham Tower. NR3 —5H 13
Mark Lemmon Clo. NR4 —4F 33
Markshall Farm Rd. NR14
　　　　—6A 34
Markshall La. NR14 —6D 34
Marland Rd. NR8 —3G 5
Marlborough Ct. NR1 —4F 25
Marlborough Ct. NR7 —2G 15
Marlborough Rd. NR3 —1D 24
Marlingford Rd. NR9 —2D 20
(Bawburgh)
Marlingford Rd. NR9 —5A 10
(Easton)
Marlingford Way. NR9 —5A 10
Marlow Ct. NR3 —4D 14
Marl Pit La. NR5 —1D 22
Marriott Chase. NR8 —4H 5
Marriott Clo. NR2 —2B 24
Marriott's Way. NR8 & NR5
　　　　—3H 5
Marryat Rd. NR7 —5H 15
Marshall Clo. NR5 —1C 22
Marshall Clo. NR10 —2G 9
Marshall Rd. NR3 —4A 14
Marsh Rd. NR12 —2C 40
Marston La. NR4 —3G 33
Marston Moor. NR7 —1E 27
Martin Clo. NR7 —3G 15
Martineau La. NR1 —2E 35
(in two parts)
Marwood Clo. NR9 —4C 30
Mary Chapman Clo. NR7
　　　　—2E 27
Mary Chapman Ct. NR3 —3B 2
Mary Chapman Ho. NR7
　　　　—1H 23
Mary Conner Ho. NR2 —5G 23
(off Elizabeth Fry Rd.)
Mason Rd. NR6 —3B 14
Massingham Rd. NR3 —6D 14
Matlock Rd. NR1 —4G 25
Maud St. NR2 —3A 24
May Clo. NR18 —3C 36
Mayes Clo. NR5 —1C 22
Mayfield Av. NR3 —3A 14
Meadow Brook Clo. NR1
　　　　—6D 24
Meadow Clo. NR5 —5B 12
Meadow Clo. NR6 —2H 13
Meadow Clo. NR9 —5C 30
Meadow Clo. NR14 —1G 35
Meadow Dri. NR12 —3C 40
Meadow Farm Dri. NR4 —5D 32
Meadow Gdns. NR6 —1E 15
Meadow La. NR7 —3C 26
Meadow Rise Av. NR2 —5H 23
Meadow Rise. NR2 —5H 23
Meadow Rise Rd. NR2 —5H 23
Meadow Rd. NR5 —5B 12
Meadowsweet. NR10 —2F 7
Meadow Vale. NR5 —4B 12
Meadow View. NR13 —3F 29
Meadow Way. NR6 —2G 13
Meadow Way. NR10 —2F 7
Meadow Way. NR14 —5C 38
Meadway. NR4 —4D 32

Medeswell Clo. NR13 —2E 29
Melrose Rd. NR4 —6H 23
Melton Clo. NR18 —2C 36
Melton Ct. NR9 —4C 30
Melton Dri. NR8 —4H 5
Melton Ga. NR18 —3C 36
Melton Rd. NR18 —3C 36
Mendham Clo. NR1 —1D 34
Merchants Ct. NR3 —2C 2
Merchant Way. NR6 —3A 14
Meredith Rd. NR6 —1F 13
Merlin Av. NR7 —3G 15
Merlin Clo. NR12 —2C 40
Merlin M. NR7 —3H 15
Merrow Gdns. NR4 —2G 33
Merton Rd. NR2 —2H 23
Metcalf Clo. NR3 —6G 13
Meteor Clo. NR6 —6C 8
Mews, The. NR13 —1G 29
Mews, The. NR2 —5B 24
Middle Rd. NR13 —6F 17
Middleton Av. NR8 —3B 14
Middleton Clo. NR9 —5C 30
Middleton Cres. NR5 —5A 12
Middleton's La. NR6 —3F 13
Middleton's La. NR6 —3F 13
Middleton St. NR18 —4C 36
Midland St. NR2 —2B 24
Midland Wlk. NR2 —2B 24
Mile Cross La. NR6 —3A 14
Mile Cross Rd. NR3 —6A 14
Mile End Clo. NR4 —6H 23
Mile End Rd. NR4 —6H 23
Milestone Clo. NR5 —5A 12
Milford Rd. NR2 —4A 24
Mill Clo. NR1 —6D 24
Mill Clo. NR9 —5C 30
Mill Clo. NR13 —3G 19
Mill Clo. NR14 —3B 38
Millcroft. NR3 —6D 14
Millcroft Clo. NR5 —6G 11
Miller's Breck. NR8 —4G 5
Millers La. NR3 —6C 14
Millers Way. NR10 —1G 7
Mill Gdns. NR10 —1G 7
Mill Hill Rd. NR2 —4A 24
Mill La. NR3 —1D 24
Mill La. NR3 —1G 7
(Horsford)
Mill La. NR10 —1B 8
(Horsham St Faith)
Mill La. NR13 —3B 28
Mill La. NR14 —1G 39
Mill Rd. NR9 —5C 30
(Hethersett)
Mill Rd. NR9 —1D 30
(Little Melton)
Mill Rd. NR13 —3F 19
Mills Clo. NR8 —4F 5
Mill St. NR10 —1B 8
Millway. NR18 —2C 36
Milton Clo. NR1 —6D 24
Milverton Rd. NR1 —6D 24
Minion Clo. NR7 —1E 27
Mitchell Ct. NR5 —1A 22
Mitre Ct. NR3 —4H 13
Mokyll Croft. NR8 —4G 5
Monastery, The. NR3
　　　　—3D 24 (3C 2)
Mons Av. NR1 —1F 25
Montcalm Rd. NR2 —2G 25
Mont Cross. NR8 —4G 5
Montgomery Clo. NR5 —2A 22
Montrose Ct. NR7 —1E 27
Moore Av. NR6 —3E 15
Moorland Clo. NR7 —5F 15
Moors, The. NR7 —3A 6
Morello Clo. NR4 —4F 23
Morgan Way. NR5 —1A 22
Morley St. NR3 —1E 25
Mornington Rd. NR2 —5H 23
Morris Clo. NR5 —1B 22
Morse Av. NR1 —2H 25
Morse Clo. NR13 —4F 29
Morse Rd. NR1 —2H 25
Mossfield Clo. NR1 —1G 25
Mottram Clo. NR5 —3E 23
Motum Rd. NR5 —2D 22
Mounteney Clo. NR8 —3E 15
Mountergate. NR1
　　　　—4D 24 (5D 3)
Mountergate Rd. NR1
　　　　—4D 24 (4D 2)
Mountfield Av. NR6 —3G 13
Mt. Pleasant. NR2 —5A 24
Mt. Surrey. NR18 —2D 36

Mousehold Av. NR3 —1E 25
Mousehold Ho. NR1 —3G 25
Mousehold La. NR7 —4F 15
Mousehold St. NR3 —1E 25
Mulberry Clo. NR3 —3A 2
Mulberry Ct. NR8 —3E 5
Munnings Rd. NR7 —5A 16
Muriel Kenny Ct. NR9 —5C 30
Muriel Rd. NR2 —5H 23
Murrayfield Rd. NR6 —2A 14
Music Ho. La. NR1
　　　　—4E 25 (6E 3)
Musley Ct. NR2 —6A 24
Muspole St. NR3 —2C 24 (2B 2)
Myrtle Av. NR8 —3A 12
Myrtle Rd. NR9 —4C 30

Naber Furlong. NR8 —2H 5
Nanhams Ct. NR2 —5A 3
Napier Pl. NR2 —2B 24
Naseby Way. NR7 —2E 27
Nasmith Rd. NR4 —1F 33
Naylor Rd. NR3 —6G 13
Nelonde Dri. NR18 —3D 36
Nelson Clo. NR9 —4F 31
Nelson Ct. NR4 —5E 23
Nelson St. NR2 —2A 24
Netherwood Grn. NR1 —1E 35
Neville Clo. NR7 —4E 15
Neville Rd. NR7 —4E 15
Neville St. NR2 —4B 24
Newatch La. NR14 —1F 39
Newbegin Clo. NR1 —2H 25
Newbegin Rd. NR1 —2G 25
Newcastle Clo. NR7 —1E 27
Newfound Dri. NR4 —2D 32
Newman Rd. NR13 —1E 17
Newmarket Rd. NR2
　　　　—6A 24 (8A 3)
Newmarket Rd. NR4 —3C 32
Newmarket St. NR2 —5B 24
New Mills Yd. NR3
　　　　—2C 24 (3A 2)
New Rd. NR9 —3E 21
(Bawburgh)
New Rd. NR9 —5B 30
(Hethersett)
Newton Clo. NR4 —2A 34
Newton Clo. NR14 —1G 35
Neylond Cres. NR6 —1F 13
Nicholas Ct. NR3 —6D 14
(off Magdalen Rd.)
Nightingale Clo. NR6 —1F 13
Nightingale Cotts. NR1 —6E 25
Nightingale Dri. NR8 —4E 5
Nightingale La. NR3 —1D 24
Nile St. NR2 —2A 24
Ninham St. NR1 —6D 24
Nobel Cres. NR12 —3A 40
Noble Clo. NR7 —6A 16
Noot All. NR5 —2C 22
Norfolk Rd. NR4 —5D 22
Norfolk St. NR2 —4B 24
Norfolk Ter. NR4 —6F 23
Norgate Rd. NR4 —6F 23
Norgate Way. NR8 —5H 5
Normandie Tower. NR1 —7E 3
Norman Dri. NR6 —1D 14
Norman Rd. NR6 —6D 14
Normans Bldgs. NR1
　　　　—4D 24 (5D 3)
Norris Ct. NR3 —3C 2
Northcote Rd. NR3 —1D 24
Northfield Clo. NR18 —2C 36
Northfield Gdns. NR18 —2C 36
Northfield La. NR18 —2C 36
Northfields. NR4 —1F 33
N. Gage Clo. NR7 —3H 15
Northgate. NR6 —2G 13
Northgate. NR13 —4E 17
N. Park Av. NR4 —4F 23
Northside. NR7 —3E 27
North St. NR13 —1G 29
Northumberland St. NR2
　　　　—2A 24
Northview Rd. NR5 —6D 12
N. Walsham Rd. NR6 & NR12
　　　　—3E 15
N. Walsham Rd. NR12 —4H 9
Norton Dri. NR4 —2H 33
Norvic Dri. NR4 —1F 33
Norwich Airport. NR6 —6A 8
Norwich Airport Ind. Est. NR6
　　　　—1A 14
Norwich Bus. Pk. NR4 —2C 34

Norwich Comn. NR18 —2G 37
Norwich Rd. NR4 —6H 33
Norwich Rd. NR5 —4C 12
Norwich Rd. NR6 —6C 30
Norwich Rd. NR10 —2A 8
Norwich Rd. NR12 —6A 40
Norwich Rd. NR13 —1G 17
(Rackheath)
Norwich Rd. NR13 —4G 17
(Thorpe End)
Norwich Rd. NR14 —1B 38
Norwich Rd. NR18 —4D 36
Norwich Southern By-Pass. NR9,
 NR5 & NR4 —4A 10
Norwich Southern By-Pass. NR14
 —6B 34
Notridge Rd. NR5 —2B 22
Notykin St. NR5 —1B 22
Nurseries Av. NR13 —3G 29
Nursery Clo. NR6 —2F 13
Nursery Gdns. NR11 —1H 29
Nursery La. NR8 —3A 12
Nutfield Clo. NR4 —2F 33
Nutwood Clo. NR8 —3G 5

Oak Av. NR7 —1C 26
Oak Av. NR14 —4C 38
Oak Clo. NR5 —5A 12
Oak Clo. NR9 —4D 30
Oakcroft Dri. NR14 —3B 38
Oakdale Rd. NR13 —4F 29
Oakfields Clo. NR4 —3F 33
Oakfields Rd. NR4 —3E 33
Oak Gro. NR10 —2G 7
Oakhill. NR13 —4F 29
Oak Ho. NR5 —1H 21
Oaklands. NR8 —3E 5
Oaklands. NR14 —2B 38
Oaklands Dri. NR4 —2D 32
Oak La. NR6 & NR3 —4C 14
Oak Lodge. NR7 —4H 25
Oak's La. NR13 —4H 27
Oak St. NR3 —2C 24 (1A 2)
Oaktree Dri. NR7 —5G 15
Oak Wood. NR13 —2G 29
Octagon Dri. NR3
 —2D 24 (2C 2)
Ogden Clo. NR18 —4D 36
Old Bank of England Ct. NR7
 —4C 2
Old Barge Yd. NR1
 —4E 25 (6E 3)
Old Farm La. NR3 —6A 14
Old Grove Ct. NR3 —5C 14
Old Hall Clo. NR14 —1G 35
Oldhall Rd. NR4 —4D 32
Old Lakenham Hall Dri. NR1
 —2D 34
Old Mill Rd. NR14 —3B 38
Old Norwich Rd. NR10 —4A 8
Old Palace Rd. NR2 —1A 24
Old Post Office Ct. NR2 —4C 2
Old Post Office Yd. NR2
 —3D 24 (4C 2)
Old Rectory Clo. NR7 —3B 26
Old Warren. NR8 —3G 5
Old Watton Rd. NR4 —4B 22
Olive Clo. NR5 —5D 12
Olive Cres. NR10 —1F 7
Olive Rd. NR5 —5C 12
One Post All. NR2 —6B 3
Onley St. NR2 —5A 24
Opie St. NR1 —3D 24 (4C 2)
Orchard Bank. NR8 —5H 5
Orchard Clo. NR7 —1H 25
Orchard Clo. NR13 —4F 19
Orchard Dri. NR6 —4E 13
Orchard Rd. NR10 —1G 9
Orchard St. NR2 —2B 24
Orchard Way. NR9 —4D 30
Orchard Way. NR18 —4C 36
Orford Hill. NR1 —5C 3
Orford Pl. NR1 —5C 3
Orford St. NR1 —5C 3
Orford Yd. NR1 —4D 24 (5C 3)
Orchid Clo. NR4 —5E 23
Orwell Clo. NR18 —3E 37
Orwell Rd. NR2 —6B 24
Osbert Clo. NR1 —3D 34
Osborne Ct. NR2 —6A 24
Osborne Rd. NR4 —6B 24
Osprey Clo. NR12 —1C 40
Oulton Rd. NR6 —2B 14
Oval Av. NR5 —6D 12
Oval Rd. NR5 —6D 12

Overbury Rd. NR6 —3H 13
Overstone Ct. NR6 —1E 15
Oxford St. NR2 —4B 24
Oxnead Rd. NR3 —5A 14

Paddocks, The. NR6 —1E 15
Paddock St. NR2 —1B 24
Paddock, The. NR6 —6E 9
Paddock, The. NR14 —1F 35
Padgate. NR13 —4E 17
Page Clo. NR14 —5C 38
Page Rd. NR3 —6G 13
Page Rd. NR13 —3E 29
Pages Clo. NR18 —5C 36
Paine Rd. NR7 —1A 26
Palace St. NR3 —3D 24 (3D 2)
Palgrave Clo. NR8 —4E 5
Palm Clo. NR18 —3C 36
Palmer Clo. NR3 —5B 14
Palmer Rd. NR3 —5B 14
Palmer Rd. NR13 —1G 17
Palmers Yd. NR1 —5C 3
Paradise Pl. NR1
 —4D 24 (6D 3)
Paragon Pl. NR2 —3B 24
Parana Clo. NR7 —2H 15
Parana Clo. NR7 —2H 15
Parana Rd. NR7 —2H 15
Park Clo. NR6 —2D 14
Park Clo. NR5 —5C 30
Park Dri. NR4 —5G 23
Park Dri. NR9 —5C 30
Parker Clo. NR13 —3D 28
Parker Rd. NR2 —4A 24
Parkers Clo. NR9 —5B 10
Parkers Clo. NR18 —2C 36
Parkland Cres. NR6 —4E 15
Parkland Rd. NR6 —4E 15
Parklands. NR8 —3G 11
Park La. NR2 —3A 24
Park La. NR13 —4D 18
Park La. NR18 —6D 36
Park Rd. NR10 —3F 9
Park Rd. NR12 —4A 40
Parkside Dri. NR6 —2D 14
Park Way. NR7 —2F 13
Parliament St. NR7 —1E 27
Parmenter Rd. NR4 —6G 23
Parr Rd. NR3 —6H 13
Parsonage Sq. NR2 —4C 2
Parsons Mead. NR4 —2G 33
Partridge Way. NR6 —3B 14
Paston Ct. NR3 —5A 14
Paston Way. NR7 —5B 16
Patricia Rd. NR1 —6C 24
Patteson Clo. NR4 —4D 32
Patteson Rd. NR3 —1C 24
Peacock St. NR3
 —2D 24 (1C 2)
Pearcefield . NR3 —5D 14
Peck Clo. NR5 —1H 21
Peckover Rd. NR4 —6F 23
Peddars Way. NR8 —3G 5
Peel M. NR3 —3A 2
Pelham Rd. NR3 —6C 14
Pembrey Clo. NR3 —4C 14
Pembroke Rd. NR2 —4A 24
Pendlesham Rise. NR8 —3H 5
Penn Clo. NR8 —5G 5
Penn Gro. NR3 —6B 14
Penn Rd. NR8 —5G 5
Pennyroyal. NR6 —2C 14
Penryn Clo. NR4 —4F 23
Penshurst M. NR4 —2G 33
Percival Clo. NR4 —5F 23
Peregrine Clo. NR7 —3H 15
Peregrine M. NR7 —3H 15
Peregrine Rd. NR7 —3H 15
Perrings. NR18 —2C 36
Peterkin Rd. NR4 —3B 34
Peterson Rd. NR3 —5H 13
Pettus Rd. NR4 —6F 23
Peverell Rd. NR5 —2B 22
Phelps Rd. NR7 —2C 26
Philadelphia La. NR3 —6H 13
Philip Ford Way .NR18 —6D 36
Pigg La. NR3 —3D 24 (3D 2)
Pigot La. NR14 —3C 38
Pilling Pk. Rd. NR1 —2G 25
Pilling Rd. NR7 —2A 26
Pimpernell Rd. NR10 —1D 6
Pinder Clo. NR3 —6H 13
Pinder Rd. NR3 —6H 13
Pine Clo. NR4 —6H 23
Pine Clo. NR7 —4A 16

Pine Loke. NR14 —3A 38
Pine Rd. NR7 —6B 16
Pinetrees Bus. Pk. NR7 —4A 16
Pinewood Clo. NR6 —3G 13
Pioneer Rd. NR6 —1F 15
Piper Rd. NR7 —6B 16
Pippin Grn. NR4 —4F 23
Pitchford Rd. NR5 —3D 22
Pitt St. NR3 —2C 24 (1B 2)
Plaford Rd. NR7 —5F 15
Plantation Dri. NR7 —4A 16
Plantation Rd. NR6 —1F 13
Plantation Rd. NR13 —1G 29
Plantation, The. NR2 —5A 24
Plantsman Clo. NR2 —6A 24
Players Way. NR6 —1D 14
Pleasant Clo. NR6 —2E 13
Plumstead Rd. NR7 —1H 25
Plumstead Rd. NR13 —1G 19
 (Blofield)
Plumstead Rd. NR13 —5E 17
 (Thorpe End)
Plumstead Rd. E. NR1 —2G 25
Pockthorpe Ga. NR3 —2F 25
Pointer Way. NR5 —2G 23
Pond Clo. NR9 —5C 30
Pond La. NR8 —5A 6
Poplar Av. NR4 —2F 33
Poplar Clo. NR5 —5A 12
Poplar Clo. NR10 —2F 7
Pople St. NR18 —4C 36
Poringland Rd. NR14 —4A 38
Porson Rd. NR7 —6H 15
Portersfield Rd. NR2 —4A 24
Porters Loke. NR7 —4F 15
Portland St. NR2 —4A 24
Portway Pl. NR2 —2B 24
Portway Sq. NR2 —2B 24
Post Mill Clo. NR7 —4E 15
Postmill Clo. NR8 —4D 36
Post Office Rd. NR13 —2C 18
Postwick La. NR13 —4C 28
Pottergate. NR2 —3B 24 (4A 2)
Pound La. NR7 —5D 16
Pound La. NR13 —2H 29
 (in two parts)
Poynt Clo. NR18 —3C 36
Press La. NR3 —6B 14
Preston Av. NR18 —6B 36
Preston Clo. NR12 —5A 40
Primrose Cres. NR7 —3D 26
Primrose Pl. NR2 —5A 24
Primrose Rd. NR1 —3F 25
Primrose Way. NR10 —2F 7
Primula Dri. NR4 —4F 23
Prince Andrew's Clo. NR6
 —2A 14
Prince Andrew's Rd. NR6
 —2A 14
Prince Edward Clo. NR7 —2C 26
Prince of Wales Rd. NR1
 —3D 24 (4D 2)
Prince Rupert Way. NR7 —6E 17
Princess Beatrice Clo. NR6
 —5E 13
Princes St. NR3 —3D 24 (3C 2)
Prior Rd. NR7 —6D 16
Priors Dri. NR6 —6G 13
Priory Clo. NR14 —4H 39
Priory Clo. NR9 —6D 30
Priory Rd. NR9 —5D 30
Priory, The. NR9 —5D 30
Priscilla Clo. NR5 —3E 23
Proctor Rd. NR6 —1E 15
Providence Pl. NR1 —3F 25
Pudding La. NR2 —5B 3
Purland Rd. NR7 —5A 16
Purtingay Clo. NR4 —2H 33
Pyehurn La. NR10 —2F 7
Pyehurn M. NR8 —2H 5
Pye's Yd. NR3 —2D 24 (2D 2)
Pyrford Dri. NR4 —2G 33

Quaker La. NR12 —4D 8
Quakers La. NR3 —1B 2
Quay Side. NR3 —2D 24 (3D 2)
Quebec Clo. NR4 —4D 32
Quebec Rd. NR1 —2H 25
Queen Elizabeth Clo. NR3 —2E 2
Queens Clo. NR4 —6H 23
Queen's Rd. NR1 —5C 24 (7B 3)
Queen's Rd. NR9 —4D 30
Queen St. NR2 —3D 24 (4C 2)
Queen St. NR18 —5D 36
Queensway. NR3 —3C 36

Quinton Gurney Ho. NR4
 —6G 33

Racecourse Rd. NR7 —6B 16
Rachel Clo. NR5 —4D 22
Rackham Rd. NR3 —5C 14
Radcliffe Rd. NR8 —3H 5
Raglan St. NR2 —3B 24
Railway Cotts. NR1 —3F 25
Rainsborough Rise. NR7 —6E 17
Raleigh Ct. NR1 —5D 3
Ramblers, The. NR14 —1A 38
Rampant Horse St. NR2
 —4C 24 (5B 3)
Ramsey Clo. NR4 —6F 23
Randle Grn. NR5 —1F 23
Randolf Rd. NR1 —2D 34
Rangoon Clo. NR7 —2H 15
Ranson Rd. NR1 —4G 25
Ranworth Rd. NR5 —2E 23
Ranworth Rd. NR13 —4H 19
Rattle Row. NR18 —4C 36
Raven Yd. NR1 —5D 3
Rawley Rd. NR5 —1B 22
Raymond Clo. NR6 —1G 13
Raymond Rd. NR6 —1F 13
Raynham St. NR2 —1B 24
Rayns Clo. NR6 —2E 15
Recorder Rd. NR1
 —3E 25 (4E 2)
Recreation Ground Rd. NR7
 —3F 15
Recreation Rd. NR2 —4H 23
Recreation Rd. NR9 —5C 30
Rectory Ct. NR3 —5C 14
Rectory La. NR9 —1D 30
Rectory La. NR14 —5D 38
Red Bri. La. NR5 —5D 12
Redcliffe Way. NR13 —3D 28
Red Cottage Clo. NR3 —5H 13
Redfern Clo. NR7 —6B 16
Redfern Rd. NR7 —6B 16
Red Lion St. NR1
 —4D 24 (6C 3)
Redwell St. NR2 —3D 24 (3C 2)
Redwing Gdns. NR10 —3G 9
Reeder's La. NR14 —6G 39
Reepham Rd. NR6 —2G 13
Reepham Rd. NR10 —1G 5
Regina Rd. NR1 —5C 24 (7B 3)
Renson Clo. NR6 —3B 14
Reve Cres. NR13 —4F 19
Reydon Clo. NR5 —2B 22
Rhond, The. NR12 —3B 40
Rice Way. NR7 —5H 15
Richardson Cres. NR9 —4B 30
Richenda Clo. NR5 —3E 23
Richmond Rd. NR5 —6H 11
Rider Haggard Rd. NR7 —6H 15
Ridgeway, The. NR1 —1G 25
Ridings, The. NR4 —3E 33
Ridings, The. NR14 —3B 38
Rigby Clo. NR14 —3D 38
Rigbys Ct. NR2 —4A 2
Rightup La. NR18 —5E 37
 (in two parts)
Riley Clo. NR7 —6A 16
Rimington Rd. NR7 —3F 15
Ringers Clo. NR18 —3E 37
Ringland La. NR8 —2C 10
 (Costessey)
Ringland La. NR8 —4A 4
 (Ringland)
Ringland Rd. NR9 —4A 10
Ringland Rd. NR8 —5B 4
Ringland Rd. NR9 —4A 10
Ring Rd. NR7 —3F 15
Ringwood Clo. NR9 —1E 31
Ripley Clo. NR2 —4G 23
Riseway. NR11 —1G 25
Riverdene M. NR8 —2H 5
River La. NR3 —2E 25 (1E 2)
Riverside. NR1 —4E 25 (6E 3)
Riverside Clo. NR6 —5E 13
Riverside Rd. NR1
 —3E 25 (5E 3)
Riverside Rd. NR12 —2B 40
Riverside Wlk. NR12 —2B 40
Roaches Ct. NR3 —3D 24 (3C 2)
Robberds Way. NR5 —1H 21
Robert Clo. NR18 —2D 36
Robert Gybson Way. NR3
 —3C 24 (3A 2)
Robin Hood Rd. NR4 —2B 34
Robson Rd. NR5 —3C 22

Rocelin Clo. NR3 —4D 14
Rockingham Rd. NR5 —3D 22
Rockland Dri. NR7 —3H 25
Roedich Dri. NR8 —4F 5
Rogers Clo. NR5 —2C 22
Rolleston Clo. NR5 —4D 22
Roman Dri. NR13 —4D 28
Romany Rd. NR3 —6E 15
Romany Wlk. NR14 —3C 38
Rook Dri. NR8 —3H 5
Ropemakers Row. NR3 —6B 14
Ropes Wlk. NR13 —1G 29
Rosa Clo. NR10 —3H 9
Rosalie Clo. NR6 —3A 14
Rosary Rd. NR1 —3F 25
Roseacre Clo. NR2 —1B 34
Rose Av. NR1 —4D 24 (5D 3)
Rosebay Clo. NR6 —2C 14
Roseberry Av. NR14 —4D 38
Rosebery Rd. NR3 —6C 14
Rosebery Ter. NR7 —3E 27
Rosebery Rd. NR13 —1A 28
Rosedale Cres. NR1 —4F 25
Rose La. NR1 —4D 24 (5D 3)
Rose Mary La. NR3
 —2C 24 (2B 2)
Rosemary Rd. NR7 —3G 15
Rosemary Rd. NR13 —3F 19
Rosetta Rd. NR10 —2H 9
Rose Valley. NR2 —4A 24
Roseville clo. NR1 —4G 25
Rose Wlk. NR13 —4E 29
Rose Yd. NR3 —1B 2
Rosslare. NR4 —2H 33
Rossons Rd. NR8 —4F 5
Rostwold Way. NR4 —2D 32
Rotary Cir. NR6 —5F 13
Rotary Ho. NR1 —8F 3
Rothbury Clo. NR18 —4D 36
Rothbury Rd. NR18 —4D 36
Rouen Rd. NR1 —4D 24 (5D 3)
Roundhead Ct. NR7 —2E 27
Roundtree Clo. NR5 —5G 15
Roundtree Way. NR7 —5G 15
Roundway Down. NR7 —1E 27
Round Well Rd. NR5 —6G 11
Rowan Clo. NR18 —3F 37
Rowan Ct. NR5 —6A 12
Rowan Ct. NR7 —4A 16
Rowan Gdns. NR9 —5C 30
Rowington Rd. NR1 —5C 24
Rowland Ct. NR1
 —5D 24 (8D 3)
Roxley Clo. NR7 —4C 36
Royal Arc. NR2 —5B 3
Royal Oak La. NR1 —6D 3
Rugge Dri. NR4 —1F 33
Runcton Clo. NR5 —2C 22
Runnel, The. NR5 —3A 22
Runnymede. NR3 —2C 2
Rupert St. NR2 —5B 24
Rushmore Clo. NR7 —2F 15
Rushmore Rd. NR7 —2F 15
Ruskin Rd. NR4 —5F 23
Ruskin Rd. NR5 —6C 12
Russell Av. NR7 —4F 15
Russell Av. NR10 —2G 9
Russell St. NR2 —2A 24
Russell Ter. NR14 —1G 35
Russell Way. NR18 —5D 36
Russet Gro. NR4 —4F 23
Rustens Mnr. Rd. NR18 —3D 36
Rutland St. NR2 —5B 24
Rydal Clo. NR3 —5D 22
Rye Av. NR3 —3A 14
Rye Clo. NR3 —3A 14
Ryrie Ct. NR3 —1G 33

Sadler Rd. NR6 —6G 7
Saffron Sq. NR3 —4C 14
St Alban's Rd. NR1 —6C 24
St Andrews Av. NR7 —3D 26
St Andrews Clo. NR7 —3D 26
St Andrews Clo. NR14 —4D 38
St Andrew's Clo. NR13 —4F 33
St Andrews Dri. NR4 —3F 33
St Andrews Hill. NR2
 —3D 24 (4C 2)
St Andrews Plain. NR3 —3C 2
St Andrew's Rd. NR6 —1E 13
St Andrews Sq. NR7 —3E 27
St Andrews St. NR2
 —3C 24 (4B 2)
St Annes Rd. NR14 —4D 38

St Ann La. NR1 —4E **25** (6E **3**)
St Augustines St. NR3 —1C **24** (1B **2**)
St Bartholomews Clo. NR2 —1A **24**
St Benedicts St. NR2 —3B **24** (3A **2**)
St Catherine Clo. NR1 —5D **24** (7C **3**)
St Catherines Clo. NR1 —7C **3**
St Catherines Plain. NR1 —8D **3**
St Catherine's Rd. NR7 —1C **26**
St Clements All. NR3 —2C **2**
St Clements Hill. NR3 —6D **14**
St Clements Way. NR13 —3E **29**
St Crispins Rd. NR3 —2C **24** (1A **2**)
St Davids Dri. NR7 —5E **17**
St David's Rd. NR9 —6C **30**
St Edmund Clo. NR14 —2A **38**
St Edmund's Clo. NR6 —6F **13**
St Edmund's Clo. NR8 —2A **12**
St Edmund's Rise. NR8 —5F **5**
St Edmund's Rd. NR8 —4F **5**
St Edmund's Way. NR14 —1H **39**
St Faiths La. NR1 —3D **24** (4D **2**)
St Faiths Rd. NR6 —3C **14**
St Georges All. NR3 —2B **2**
St Georges St. NR3 —2C **24** (2B **2**)
St Giles St. NR2 —3C **24** (4A **2**)
St Giles Ter. NR2 —4A **2**
St Gregory's All. NR2 —4B **2**
St Helena Way. NR10 —1F **7**
St Helen's Sq. NR1 —2E **25** (2E **2**)
St James Clo. NR3 —2E **25** (1F **2**)
St John Maddermarket. NR2 —3C **24** (4B **2**)
St John's All. NR2 —4B **2**
St John's Clo. NR1 —1D **34**
St John's Clo. NR9 —6C **30**
St Johns St. NR1 —4E **25** (5E **3**)
St Julians All. NR1 —4D **24** (6D **3**)
St Laurence Av. NR13 —3E **29**
St Lawrence Clo. NR2 —3A **2**
St Lawrence Dri. NR4 —2D **32**
St Lawrence La. NR2 —3C **24** (4B **2**)
St Lawrence Lit. Steps. NR2 —3A **2**
St Leonards Dri. NR18 —2D **36**
St Leonards Rd. NR1 —3F **25**
St Margarets All. NR2 —3A **2**
St Margarets Dri. NR7 —2G **15**
St Margarets Gdns. NR12 —1C **40**
St Margarets M. NR12 —3B **40**
St Margarets St. NR2 —3C **24** (3A **2**)
St Martins -at- Palace Plain. NR3 —2D **24** (2D **2**)
St Martin's Clo. NR3 —1C **24**
St Martin's La. NR3 —2C **24** (2A **2**)
St Martin's Rd. NR3 —1C **24**
St Mary's All. NR3 —2B **2**
St Mary's Clo. NR10 —2B **8**
St Mary's Clo. NR12 —3A **40**
St Mary's Clo. NR13 —6A **18**
St Mary's Clo. NR14 —4H **39**
St Marys Gro. NR7 —2H **15**
St Mary's Ho. NR3 —2C **24** (2B **2**)
St Mary's Plain. NR3 —2C **24** (2B **2**)
St Mary's Rd. NR3 —1C **24**
St Marys Rd. NR14 —4D **38**
St Matthews Rd. NR1 —3E **25** (4F **2**)
St Michael at Pleas Ct. NR2 —3D **2**
St Michael's Ter. NR1 —2F **25**
St Michaels Way. NR13 —5H **29**
St Mildreds Rd. NR5 —3C **22**
St Miles All. NR3 —3B **2**
St Olaves Rd. NR3 —1D **24**
St Paul's Clo. NR6 —2H **13**
St Paul's Clo. NR10 —1G **7**
St Pauls Opening. NR3 —2D **24** (1D **2**)
St Pauls Sq. NR3 —1D **2**
St Peters Clo. NR4 —3E **33**
St Peters St. NR2 —3C **24** (4B **2**)
St Peter's Way. NR10 —2G **9**
St Philips Clo. NR2 —3A **24**
St Philips Rd. NR2 —3A **24**
St Saviours All. NR3 —1C **2**
St Saviours La. NR3 —2D **24** (2C **2**)
Saints Ct. NR1 —6C **3**
St Simon Ct. NR3 —3D **2**
St Stephens Rd. NR1 —5C **24** (8A **3**)
St Stephens Sq. NR1 —5C **24** (7A **3**)
St Stephens St. NR1 —4C **24** (6B **3**)
St Swithins All. NR2 —3A **2**
St Swithins Rd. NR2 —3C **24** (3A **2**)
St Thomas Dri. NR18 —6E **37**
St Thomas Rd. NR2 —3H **23**
St Vedast St. NR1 —3E **25** (4E **2**)
St Walstans Clo. NR5 —6G **11**
St Walstan's Clo. NR8 —5G **5**
St Walstan's Rd. NR8 —4G **5**
St Wensum St. NR3 —2C **2**
St Williams Way. NR7 —1H **25**
Saker Clo. NR7 —1E **27**
Sale Rd. NR7 —5A **16**
Salhouse Rd. NR7 —6G **15**
Salhouse Rd. NR7 & NR13 —4B **16**
Salhouse Rd. NR12 —5A **40**
Salhouse Rd. NR13 —1C **18**
Salhouse Rd. Ind. Est. NR7 —5H **15**
Salisbury Rd. NR1 —4G **25**
Salter Av. NR4 —4F **23**
Samson Rd. NR6 —3G **13**
Samuel Rd. NR1 —1G **25**
Sandhole La. NR13 —2B **18**
Sandholme Clo. NR1 —1G **25**
Sandringham Ct. NR2 —8A **3**
Sandringham Rd. NR2 —3A **24**
Sandy La. NR4 & NR1 —2C **34**
Sandy La. NR8 —5F **5**
Sandy La. NR9 —2A **10**
Saracen Rd. NR6 —1G **13**
Sarah Williman Clo. NR5 —4D **22**
Saunders Ct. NR1 —3F **25**
Savery Clo. NR5 —3C **22**
Sawmill Clo. NR18 —3C **36**
Sawyers Clo. NR5 —6H **11**
Saxonfields. NR14 —5C **38**
Sayers St. NR2 —2B **24**
Scarlet Rd. NR4 —2C **34**
Scarnell Rd. NR5 —3E **23**
Sceptre Clo. NR6 —4H **13**
School Av. NR7 —3C **26**
School La. NR2 —4C **2**
School La. NR7 —3E **15** (Sprowston)
School La. NR7 —3A **26** (Thorpe St Andrew, in three parts)
School La. NR9 —1F **31**
School Rd. NR8 —4A **6**
School Rd. NR13 —4C **18**
School Ter. NR14 —1G **35**
Scotch Hill Rd. NR8 —4F **5**
Scott Rd. NR1 —4G **25**
Scott's Ct. NR1 —6C **3**
Scott's Yd. NR1 —7D **3**
Seabrook Ct. NR5 —2B **22**
Seaforth Dri. NR8 —5H **5**
Seaman Tower. NR3 —5H **13**
Seates, The. NR8 —3G **5**
Sedman Wlk. NR5 —1B 22 (off Rawley Rd.)
Sego Vale. NR8 —5H **5**
Seppings Way. NR13 —4E **17**
Seton Rd. NR8 —4H **5**
Sewell Rd. NR3 —6D **14**
Shack La. NR13 —1E **29**
Shakespeare Way. NR8 —5G **5**
Sheep Meadow Clo. NR5 —6A **12**
Sheffield Rd. NR18 —2D **36**
Shelley Dri. NR8 —5G **5**
Shepherd Clo. NR5 —4E **23**
Shepherds Clo. NR10 —2F **7**
Shepherd Way. NR8 —3H **5**
Sherbourne Pl. NR1 —4E **25** (7E **3**)
Sheridan Clo. NR8 —5A **6**
Sherwell Rd. NR6 —1F **13**
Sherwood Rd. NR4 —2B **34**
Sherwyn Ho. NR3 —2C **24** (2B **2**)
Shilito Rd. NR13 —1H **29**
Shipfield. NR3 —5E **15**
Shipstone Rd. NR3 —1C **24**
Shires, The. NR8 —3A **6**
Shooters Clo. NR8 —4G **5**
Shop La. NR9 —4F **31**
Shorncliffe Av. NR3 —6A **14**
Shorncliffe Clo. NR3 —6B **14**
Shotesham Rd. NR14 —6B **38**
Shrublands. NR2 —3A 24 (off Heigham Rd.)
Shrublands, The. NR10 —1G **7**
Sidell Clo. NR4 —4D **32**
Sidney Rd. NR8 —3A **12**
Sienna M. NR1 —2G **25**
Sigismund Rd. NR1 —6C **24**
Silfield Av. NR18 —6E **37**
Silfield Rd. NR18 —6D **36**
Silkfields. NR3 —2A **2**
Silver Rd. NR3 —6D **14** (1E **2**)
Silver St. NR3 —1D **24**
Singer Ct. NR3 —2C **2**
Skedge Way. NR13 —4E **19**
Skelton Rd. NR7 —1H **25**
Skoner Rd. NR5 —1C **22**
Skye Clo. NR5 —1B **22**
Slade La. NR14 —1G **39**
Sleaford Grn. NR3 —5B **14**
Smeat St. NR5 —2C **22**
Smee La. NR13 —1G **27**
Smithdale Rd. NR5 —6C **12**
Smithfield Rd. NR1 —6D **24**
Smithson Clo. NR18 —3D **36**
Smock Mill Loke. NR18 —3C **36**
Snowberry Clo. NR8 —3E **5**
Softley Dri. NR4 —1D **32**
Sole Clo. NR10 —2G **7**
Soleme Rd. NR3 —5H **13**
Somerleyton Gdns. NR2 —4B **24**
Somerleyton St. NR2 —4B **24**
Somerset Way. NR8 —4D **4**
Sonya Ter. NR1 —2G **25**
Sorrel Ho. NR5 —1B **22**
Sotherton Rd. NR4 —6G **23**
South Av. NR7 —4B **26**
South Croft. NR9 —5C **30**
Southerwood. NR6 —2C **14**
Southfield La. NR13 —1E **19**
S. Gage Clo. NR7 —3A **16**
Southgate La. NR1 —5E **25** (8E **3**)
S. Hill Clo. NR7 —1C **26**
S. Park Av. NR4 —6F **23**
South Wlk. NR13 —5E **17**
Southwell Rd. NR1 —5C **24**
S. Wood Dri. NR14 —2A **38**
Sovereign Way. NR3 —2D **24** (1C **2**)
Sparhawk Av. NR7 —3H **15**
Sparhawk Clo. NR7 —3H **15**
Spar Rd. NR6 —2B **14**
Speke St. NR2 —2H **23**
Spelman Rd. NR2 —5H **23**
Spencer Rd. NR6 —2B **14**
Spencer St. NR3 —1D **24**
Spigot Rd. NR18 —6B **36**
Spindle Rd. NR6 —3C **14**
Spink's La. NR18 —2G **37** (in three parts)
Spinney Clo. NR7 —1C **26**
Spinney Rd. NR7 —1B **26**
Spinney, The. NR7 —2E **27**
Spitalfields. NR1 —2F **25**
Spitfire Rd. NR6 —1B **14**
Spixworth Rd. NR6 —4D **14**
Spixworth Rd. NR10 —2B **8**
Springbank. NR1 —1D **34**
Springdale Cres. NR13 —3D **28**
Springdale Rd. NR13 —3D **28**
Springfield Rd. NR7 —5A **16**
Springfield Rd. NR8 —3F **5**
Springfields. NR14 —4C **38**
Springwood. NR8 —4H **5**
Sprowston Rd. NR3 —6D **14**
Spur La. NR14 —2C **38**
Spynke Rd. NR3 —4A **14**
Square, The. NR4 —5D **22**
Squire's Haven. NR1 —4F **25**
Stacy Rd. NR3 —1D **24**
Stafford Av. NR5 —6A **12**
Stafford St. NR2 —3H **23**
Staithe La. NR13 —4F **29**
Staitheway Rd. NR12 —3B **40**
Stalham Rd. NR12 —2C **40**
Stalham Rd. Ind. Est. NR12 —1D **40**
Stamp Office Yd. NR3 —3C **2**
Standley Ct. NR18 —4C **36**
Stanfield Rd. NR18 —5G **37**
Stanley Av. NR7 —4H **25**
Stanleys La. NR18 —6D **36**
Stanmore Clo. NR7 —3B **26**
Stanmore Rd. NR7 —3B **26**
Stannard Rd. NR4 —4G **23**
Starling Rd. NR3 —1C **24**
Statham Clo. NR4 —1A **34**
Station Cotts. NR9 —6H **31**
Station La. NR9 —4G **31** (in two parts)
Station New Rd. NR13 —4G **29**
Station Rd. NR8 —6A **6**
Station Rd. NR12 —2B **40**
Station Rd. NR13 —4F **29**
Station Rd. NR18 —5D **36**
Steepgreen Clo. NR1 —1H **25**
Steeple Chase. NR8 —3A **6**
Stepping La. NR1 —4D **24** (5D **3**)
Steps, The. NR2 —3A **24**
Stevenson Rd. NR5 —2C **22**
Steward Clo. NR18 —3E **37**
Steward St. NR3 —1D **24**
Stile La. NR18 —3C **36**
Stillington Clo. NR7 —4G **15**
Stocks Hill. NR9 —3E **21**
Stocks La. NR13 —2G **29**
Stoke Rd. NR1 —2E **35**
Stoke Rd. NR14 —3B **38**
Stone Breck. NR5 —5H **11**
Stone Bldgs. NR3 —6D **14**
Stone Ho. Clo. NR3 —5C **14**
Stonehouse Rd. NR7 —3G **15**
Stone Rd. NR3 —6B **14**
Stone Rd. NR13 —6H **29**
Stracey Rd. NR1 —4F **25**
Strangers Ct. NR2 —3C **24** (4B **2**)
Stratford Clo. NR1 —1E **35**
Stratford Cres. NR4 —2D **32**
Stratford Dri. NR1 —1D **34**
Strayground La. NR18 —6C **36**
Street, The. NR1 —6F **25**
Street, The. NR4 —5E 23 (off Square, The.)
Street, The. NR8 —3H **11** (Costessey)
Street, The. NR8 —4A **4** (Ringland)
Street, The. NR8 —4E **5** (Taverham)
Street, The. NR13 —1G **29** (Blofield)
Street, The. NR13 —3E **29** (Brundall)
Street, The. NR14 —1D **38** (Framingham Pigot)
Street, The. NR14 —3C **38** (Poringland)
Street, The. NR14 —6D **28** (Surlingham)
Street, The. NR14 —1G **35** (Trowse Newton)
Strumpshaw Rd. NR13 —4F **29**
Stuart Clo. NR9 —4D **30**
Stuart Ct. NR1 —4E **2**
Stuart Gdns. NR1 —4E **2**
Stuart Rd. NR1 —5E **25** (8F **3**)
Stylman Rd. NR5 —2B **22**
Suckling Av. NR3 —4A **14**
Suckling La. NR9 —6E **31**
Suckling La. NR14 —1E **39**
Suffield Clo. NR4 —3E **33**
Suffield Ct. NR3 —5C **14**
Suffolk Rd. NR4 —6D **22**
Suffolk Sq. NR2 —4B **24**
Suffolk Ter. NR4 —6D **22**
Suffolk Wlk. NR4 —6D **22**
Summer Dri. NR12 —1C **40**
Sumpter Rd. NR4 —6F **23**
Suncroft. NR1 —1E **35**
Sun La. NR3 —6C **14**
Sunningdale. NR4 —1H **33**
Sunny Clo. NR5 —6C **12**
Sunny Gro. NR5 —6C **12**
Sunny Hill. NR1 —1E **35**
Sunnyside Av. NR14 —4C **38**
Supple Clo. NR1 —2H **25**
Surrey Clo. NR7 —2H **15**
Surrey Gro. NR1 —4D **24** (7C **3**)
Surrey St. NR1 —4D **24** (6C **3**)
Sursham Av. NR6 —2E **15**
Sussex St. NR3 —2C **24** (1A **2**)
Suters Dri. NR8 —3H **5**
Sutherland Av. NR6 —3H **13**
Sutton La. NR18 —6B **36**
Swafield St. NR5 —2A **22**
Swale, The. NR5 —3A **22**
Swan La. NR2 —4C **2**
Swansea Rd. NR2 —4A **24**
Swansgate. NR6 —1D **14**
Swan St. NR10 —2A **8**
Swanton Rd. NR2 —1A **24**
Sweet Briar Ind. Est. NR3 —6G **13**
Sweetbriar La. NR6 —6G **9**
Sweet Briar Retail Pk. NR3 —5G **13**
Sweet Briar Rd. NR6 —1G **23**
Swinbourne Clo. NR6 —4C **14**
Swindells Clo. NR5 —5B **12**
Sycamore Av. NR18 —2E **37**
Sycamore Cres. NR2 —2G **23**
Sydney Rd. NR10 —2F **9**
Sylvan Way. NR8 —5H **5**
Sywell Clo. NR6 —1E **15**

Talbot Clo. NR18 —3D **36**
Talbot Sq. NR3 —2C **24** (1A **2**)
Taleworth Clo. NR5 —1B **22**
Tanager Clo. NR3 —4C **14**
Tanners Ct. NR3 —1B **24**
Tansy Clo. NR6 —3C **14**
Taverham Chase. NR8 —5G **5**
Taverham La. NR8 —5E **5**
Taverham Rd. NR8 —5F **5**
Taverners Sq. NR3 —1E **2**
Taylor Av. NR4 —4D **32**
Taylor Rd. NR5 —3D **22**
Taylor's Ct. NR3 —6D 14 (off Magdalen Rd.)
Taylor's La. NR6 —1C **14**
Telegraph La. E. NR1 —3F **25**
Telegraph La. W. NR1 —3F **25**
Telford Clo. NR3 —6G **13**
Templemere. NR3 —5F **15**
Temple Rd. NR3 —6D **14**
Ten Bell Ct. NR2 —3C **24** (3A **2**)
Ten Bell La. NR2 —3C **24** (4A **2**)
Tenison Ct. NR4 —2F **33**
Terence Av. NR7 —3F **15**
Terrace, The. NR1 —3F **25**
Terrace Wlk. NR1 —8D **3**
Theatre St. NR2 —4C **24** (5A **3**)
Theobald Rd. NR1 —4C **34**
Thicket, The. NR8 —3H **5**
Thirlmere. NR9 —4E **31**
Thomas Vere Rd. NR7 —2C **26**
Thompson Rd. NR7 —1C **26**
Thompsons Yd. NR3 —2D **24** (2C **2**)
Thor Clo. NR7 —2B **26**
Thor Loke. NR7 —2B **26**
Thornham Clo. NR7 —5G **15**
Thornham Dri. NR7 —5G **15**
Thornham Rd. NR7 —5G **15**
Thorn La. NR1 —4D **24** (6D **3**)
Thoroughfare Yd. NR3 —2C **2**
Thorpe Av. NR7 —1B **26**
Thorpe Clo. NR7 —2C **26**
Thorpe Hall Clo. NR7 —4H **25**
Thorpe Heights. NR1 —3F **25**
Thorpe M. NR7 —4C **26**
Thorpe Rd. NR1 —4E **25** (5F **3**)
Thor Rd. NR7 —2B **26**
Three Acre Clo. NR12 —1B **40**
Three Corner Dri. NR6 —1E **15**
Three King La. NR2 —3C **24** (4A **2**)
Three Mile La. NR5 —6A **12**
Three Score Rd. NR5 —3A **22**
Three Towers Ct. NR3 —5H **13**
Three Tuns Ct. NR1 —5D **3**
Throckmorton Yd. NR3 —1D **24**
Thunder La. NR7 —6B **16**
Thurlby Rd. NR5 —1H **21**
Thurling Loke. NR7 —6B **16**
Thurling Plain. NR7 —6B **16**
Thurlow Clo. NR5 —1H **21**
Thurston Clo. NR5 —1A **22**
Tiercel Av. NR7 —3H **15**
Tillett Ct. NR3 —5D **14**
Tillett Rd. NR3 —5D **14**

Tillett Rd. E. NR3 —5D 14
Tills Clo. NR6 —3E 15
Tills Rd. NR6 —2E 15
Timberhill. NR1 —4D 24 (5C 3)
Timothy Clo. NR1 —1G 25
Tinker's La. NR13 —6H 29
Tippett Clo. NR5 —3B 22
Toad La. NR13 —5H 17
Toftes Pl. NR5 —1C 22
Tollhouse Rd. NR5 —2F 23
Tolwin Wlk. NR3 —6E 15
Tombland. NR3 —3D 24 (3D 2)
Tombland All. NR3 —3D 2
Tottington Clo. NR5 —1A 22
Tower Clo. NR8 —3F 11
Tower Hill. NR7 —3A 26
Tower Hill. NR8 —3F 11
Towers, The. NR1 —8F 3
Town Clo. Rd. NR2 —6B 24
Town Grn. NR18 —4C 36
Town Ho. Rd. NR8 —3H 11
Townsend Rd. NR4 —2B 34
Townshend Ct. NR1 —6D 24
Toyle Rd. NR5 —2A 22
Tracey Rd. NR7 —6B 16
Trafalgar St. NR1 —5D 24 (8D 3)
Trafford Rd. NR5 —5C 24
(in two parts)
Trafford Wlk. NR12 —5A 40
Traverse St. NR3 —6C 14
Tremaine Clo. NR6 —6E 13
Trendall Rd. NR7 —3A 16
Trident Dri. NR1 —2F 25
Trilithon Clo. NR6 —5F 13
Trimming Wlk. NR8 —5H 5
Trinity St. NR2 —4B 24
Trix Rd. NR2 —5B 24
Trory St. NR2 —4B 24
Troutbeck. NR9 —4E 31
Trowse By-Pass. NR14 —2F 35
Truman Clo. NR5 —4D 22
Tuckswood Cen. NR4 —2A 34
Tuckswood La. NR4 —1B 34
Tudor Ct. NR1 —5D 24 (8D 3)
Tungate Cres. NR4 —4E 33
Tunstall Clo. NR5 —2B 22
Tunstead La. NR12 —1C 40
Tunstead Rd. NR12 —2B 40
Turner Rd. NR2 —2H 23
Turners Sq. NR1 —5D 3
Turnham Grn. NR7 —1E 27
Tusser Rd. NR8 —5H 5
Tusting Clo. NR7 —3E 15
Tuttles La. E. NR18 —2D 36
Tuttles La. W. NR18 —2A 36
Twickenham Rd. NR6 —2A 14
Two Saints Clo. NR12 —1C 40

Ullswater Dri. NR9 —4E 31
Union Pl. NR4 —5E 23
Union St. NR2 —5B 24
University Dri. NR4 —5E 23
Unthank Rd. NR2 —6H 23
Unthank Rd. NR4 —6H 23
Upgate. NR14 —4E 39
Uphalle. NR8 —4G 5
Uplands Ct. NR4 —6H 23
Up. Breckland Rd. NR5 —6A 12
Upper Clo. NR1 —3D 24 (3D 2)
Up. Goat La. NR2
—3C 24 (4B 2)

Up. Green La. NR3
—2D 24 (1C 2)
Up. King St. NR3
—3D 24 (4D 2)
Up. St Giles St. NR2
—3B 24 (4A 2)
Up. Stafford Av. NR5 —6A 12
Upton Clo. NR4 —1H 33
Upton Rd. NR4 —6H 23

Vale Clo. NR10 —2F 7
Vale Grn. NR3 —6H 13
Valentine St. NR2 —3B 24
Valley Dri., The. NR1 —6G 15
Valley Rd. NR5 —6C 12
Valleyside. NR18 —5D 36
Valley Side Rd. NR1 —1H 25
Valley View Cres. NR5 —6A 12
Valpy Av. NR3 —6H 13
Vancouver Rd. NR7 —1H 25
Varvel Av. NR7 —3H 15
Varvel Clo. NR7 —4H 15
Vauxhall St. NR2 —4B 24
Vawdrey Rd. NR8 —4A 6
Venables Clo. NR1 —2G 25
Vera St. NR3 —2G 17
Vera Rd. NR6 —3A 14
Vera Rd. NR13 —1G 17
Vicarage Clo. NR8 —2A 12
Vicarage Ct. NR7 —4F 15
Vicarage Rd. NR3 —6B 14
Vicar St. NR18 —4C 36
Victoria Clo. NR8 —5F 5
Victoria Rd. NR8 —5F 5
Victoria St. NR1 —5C 24 (7B 3)
Victoria Way. NR5 —5C 12
Vienna Appartments. NR7
—4H 25
Vincent Rd. NR1 —2F 25
Violet Rd. NR3 —6E 15
Virginia Clo. NR7 —4H 15
Vulcan Rd. Ind. Est. NR6
—2B 14
Vulcan Rd. N. NR6 —2B 14
Vulcan Rd. S. NR6 —3B 14

Waddington Ct. NR2 —2A 24
Waddington St. NR2 —2A 24
Wades Yd. NR2 —4D 2
Waggon & Horses La. NR3
—3D 24 (3C 2)
Wakefield Rd. NR5 —3D 22
Wakehurst Clo. NR4 —2G 33
Walcott Clo. NR5 —2C 22
Waldeck Rd. NR4 —6H 23
Waldegrave. NR5 —1B 22
Waldemar Av. NR7 —3B 26
Waldemar Pk. NR6 —2A 14
Wall Rd. NR3 —5D 14
Walnut Clo. NR8 —3G 5
Walnuts, The. NR4 —1A 34
Walpole St. NR2 —4B 24
Walters Rd. NR8 —5G 5
Walton Rd. NR1 —6D 24
Ward La. NR7 —6A 16
Waring Rd. NR5 —3C 22
War Memorial Cotts. NR7
—5G 15
Warnett Rd. NR7 —6A 16
Warren Av. NR6 —2H 13

Warren Clo. NR6 —3D 14
Warren, The. NR6 —3D 14
Warren, The. NR10 —1A 8
Warwick Dri. NR18 —2D 36
Warwick St. NR2 —4A 24
Wash La. NR14 —5D 38
Watering, The. NR3 —1B 24
Water La. NR3 —3C 24 (3B 2)
Water La. NR4 —2D 32
Water La. NR7 —4A 26
Water La. NR13 —6A 18
Waterloo Clo. NR10 —2A 8
Waterloo Pk. Av. NR3 —6B 14
Waterloo Pk. Clo. NR3 —6B 14
Waterloo Rd. NR3 —1C 24
Waterloo Rd. NR10 —2B 8
Waterman Rd. NR2 —2G 23
Waterside. NR1 —2E 25 (2F 2)
Waterworks Rd. NR2 —2H 23
Watkins Rd. NR4 —3B 34
Watling Rd. NR7 —1H 25
Watlings Ct. NR2 —4A 2
Watson Gro. NR2 —1A 24
Watton Rd. NR9 & NR4 —5A 20
Watts Ct. NR2 —5A 3
Waveney Clo. NR12 —1D 40
Waveney Dri. NR12 —2C 40
Waveney Rd. NR4 —5E 23
Waveney Ter. NR4 —5E 23
Waverley Rd. NR4 —1H 33
Weavers La. NR2 —6B 14
Webdell Ct. NR1 —2E 35
Webster Clo. NR5 —1C 22
Wellesley Av. N. NR1 —2G 25
Wellesley Av. S. NR1 —3G 25
Wellington La. NR2 —3B 24
Wellington Rd. NR2 —3A 24
Well Loke. NR3 —4A 14
Wellsford Rd. NR4 —2A 34
Welsford Rd. NR4 —2A 34
Wendene. NR5 —2A 22
Wenman Ct. NR5 —1A 22
Wensum Ct. NR1 —5D 3
Wensum Cres. NR6 —4E 13
Wensum St. NR3
—3D 24 (3C 2)
Wensum Valley Clo. NR6
—3E 13
Wensum Wlk. NR8 —2A 6
Wentworth Grn. NR4 —1H 33
Wessex St. NR2 —4B 24 (7A 3)
Westacre Dri. NR6 —6D 8
West Clo. NR5 —5B 12
West Croft. NR9 —5C 30
West End Av. NR8 —2F 11
West End Av. NR14 —5C 38
West End St. NR2 —2A 24
Western Av. NR7 —3B 26
Westfield Rd. NR13 —3F 29
Westgate. NR6 —2G 13
West Ga. NR18 —4C 36
Westgate Clo. NR2 —5H 23
Westgate Ct. NR18 —4C 36
West La. NR10 —3H 7
Westlegate. NR1 —4D 24 (6C 3)
Weston Clo. NR13 —3F 19
Weston Ct. NR6 —1E 15
Weston Rd. NR3 & NR6 —4B 14
Weston Wood Clo. NR7 —3B 26
Weston Wood Rd. NR7 —3B 26
West Pde. NR2 —3A 24

W. Pottergate. NR2 —3A 24
West Rd. NR5 —5B 12
West View. NR14 —6C 38
West View Rd. NR13 —1G 29
Westwick St. NR2
—2C 24 (2A 2)
Westwood Dri. NR6 —1E 13
Westwood Gdns. NR2 —2A 36
Westwood Ho. NR2 —3H 23
Wharton's La. NR18 —6C 36
Wheatfields. NR8 —3A 6
Wheatley Rd. NR2 —2G 23
Wheeler Rd. NR3 —6H 13
Wheel Rd. NR14 —5G 39
Whiffler Rd. NR3 —4H 13
Whitebeam Ct. NR5 —2E 23
White Farm La. NR7 —3H 25
Whitefriars. NR3 —2D 24 (1D 2)
White Gates. NR6 —5H 11
Whitegates Clo. NR9 —5D 30
Whitehall Rd. NR2 —4A 24
White Horse La. NR14 —3E 35
White Horse M. NR14 —1G 35
Whitehorse St. NR18 —5C 36
White Ho. Ct. NR3 —4A 14
Whitehouse Gdns. NR14
—4E 39
White Lion St. NR2
—4D 24 (5C 3)
White Rose Clo. NR5 —1E 23
Whitethorn Clo. NR6 —2C 14
White Woman La. NR6 —1E 15
Whiting Rd. NR4 —2C 34
Whitlingham La. NR7 —4C 26
Whitlingham La. NR14 —1G 35
Whitwell Rd. NR1 —2F 25
Wilberforce Rd. NR5 —3C 22
Wilby Rd. NR1 —2D 34
Wild Rd. NR3 —6C 14
Willhire Way. NR6 —1A 14
William Booth St. NR2
—4C 24 (5B 3)
William Clo. NR18 —2D 36
William Mear Gdns. NR1
—3G 25
William Peck Clo. NR10 —2F 9
William Peck Rd. NR10 —2F 9
Williamson Clo. NR7 —5H 15
William White Pl. NR1 —2F 25
Williams's Loke. NR7 —1A 26
Willis St. NR3 —2D 24 (1D 2)
Willow Clo. NR18 —3E 37
Willow La. NR2 —3C 24 (4A 2)
Wilson Rd. NR1 —4G 25
Winceby Clo. NR7 —1E 27
Winchcomb Rd. NR2 —2G 23
Windmill Clo. NR14 —5C 38
Windmill Ct. NR3 —5F 15
Windmill La. NR8 —3B 12
Windmill Rd. NR3 —5E 15
Windsor Chase. NR8 —4G 5
Windsor Rd. NR6 —1G 13
Wingate Way. NR2 —2B 24
Wingfield Rd. NR3 —1C 24
Winkles Row. NR1 —8F 3
Winners Wlk. NR8 —2A 6
Winsford Way. NR5 —6D 12
Winter Rd. NR2 —3H 23
Witard Clo. NR7 —6A 16
Witard Rd. NR7 —6A 16
Withy Way. NR8 —4H 5
Witton La. NR13 —1A 28

Woburn St. NR2 —4B 24
Wodehouse Clo. NR18 —2B 36
Wodehouse St. NR3 —1D 24
Wolfe Rd. NR1 —2G 25
Wolfson Clo. NR4 —5E 23
Womersley Clo. NR1 —2G 25
Womersley Rd. NR1 —2G 25
Woodbastwick Rd. NR13
—1F 19
Woodcock Clo. NR3 —4C 14
Woodcock Rd. NR3 —4B 14
Woodcote. NR9 —5D 30
Woodcroft Clo. NR7 —5B 16
Woodforde Rd. NR7 —5A 16
Woodgate. NR4 —4D 32
Woodgrove Pde. NR3 —5C 14
Woodham Leas. NR6 —1D 14
Wood Hill. NR8 —5G 5
Woodhill Rise. NR5 —1D 22
Woodland Clo. NR6 —1E 13
Woodland Dri. NR6 —1D 14
Woodland Dri. NR13 —5E 17
Woodland Rd. NR6 —1E 13
Woodlands. NR8 —3E 5
Woodlands Cres. NR7 —6D 16
Woodlands Rd. NR5 —5B 12
Woodrow Pl. NR1 —3G 25
Woodruff Clo. NR6 —2C 14
Woods Clo. NR9 —5C 30
Woodside Clo. NR8 —4F 5
Woodside Ct. NR1 —6E 25
Woodside Rd. NR7 —5B 16
Wood St. NR1 —5C 24 (7A 3)
Wood View Ct. NR5 —5B 12
Wood View Rd. NR6 —2F 13
Woodview Rd. NR9 —5A 10
Woodward Rd. NR3 —5A 14
Woolner's La. NR14 —1F 39
Wordsworth Rd. NR5 —3D 22
Wortham Clo. NR5 —1B 22
Wramplingham Rd. NR18
—1E 37
Wren Dro. NR1 —4F 33
Wrench Rd. NR5 —3E 23
Wrenningham Rd. NR6 —1D 14
Wrights Clo. NR3 —3C 2
Wright's Foundry Yd. NR2
—2C 24 (2B 2)
Wroxham Rd. NR3
—4F 15
Wycliffe Rd. NR4 —5F 23
Wymer St. NR2 —3A 24
Wyngates. NR13 —1H 25

Yare Valley Dri. NR4 —1D 32
Yarmouth Rd. NR7 —4H 25
Yarmouth Rd. NR13 —2E 29
Yaxley Way. NR5 —2B 22
Yelverton Clo. NR6 —2E 13
Yelverton Rd. NR14 —3E 39
Yew Ct. NR7 —3A 16
York St. NR2 —5A 24
(in two parts)

Zipfel's Ct. NR3 —1C 2
Zobel Clo. NR3 —5G 13